D1395253

PRAISE FOR
HOW GREAT LEADERS GET GREAT RESULTS

"Great leaders! Great stories! Great lessons! A wise person learns from experience—a much wiser person learns from someone else's experience. Reading *How Great Leaders Get Great Results* is a wonderful way to learn! These stories show the human side of leadership."

—Marshall Goldsmith,
executive coach and author or coeditor of 18 books;
recently named by the American Management Association
as one of 50 great thinkers and leaders

"*How Great Leaders Get Great Results* is a great resource for leaders at every level of the enterprise. Whether you want to lead in business, government, or nonprofits, this book will help you focus on results. John Baldoni's four-step process illuminates the communication imperative for the leader of the future. It's a powerful book."

—Frances Hesselbein, Chairman, Leader to Leader Institute

"Everything we do communicates something about who we are. Baldoni captures the essence of how leaders communicate by word and example who they are and what they wish to achieve. With a deft touch and highly readable stories, Baldoni illustrates the post-modern leadership skills that all leaders must demonstrate in order to succeed. This book embodies the kind of clarity and practicality that all leaders must exert to achieve lasting results."

—Mark Linder, global client leader, WPP Group

"Effective leaders communicate their ideas and strategies in ways that inspire people to support them wholeheartedly. John Baldoni's insightful book describes how the most effective leaders use 'results-oriented communications and stories' to move people and organizations forward. Baldoni has done us a great service by identifying nine great communicators, telling their stories, and highlighting the most effective communication techniques that we all can use to get better results at work."

—Paula Caproni, Ph. D, Director of Professional Development
for the Executive MBA Program, Ross School of Business
at the University of Michigan;
author of *Management Skills for Everyday Life*

"*How Great Leaders Get Great Results* is a book that all leaders will want to read. John Baldoni offers insights into how leaders can use their communications to build support for their ideas and carry them to fruition. The stories of leaders profiled in the book demonstrate that results come from people who know how to bring people together to generate results that are intended, mutually beneficial, and sustainable."

—William Phebus, Secretary/Treasurer,
Williams/Gerard Productions

"John Baldoni brings to life the great leaders of our time. Listen, watch, and learn how these individuals lead their entities to success. All the lessons are here. I recommend this book to anyone who seeks to produce results the right way."

—David J. Cichelli, Senior Vice President,
The Alexander Group, Inc.

HOW GREAT LEADERS GET GREAT RESULTS

ALSO BY JOHN BALDONI

Great Motivation Secrets of Great Leaders (2005)

Great Communication Secrets of Great Leaders (2003)

180 Ways to Walk the Motivation Talk (coauthored with Eric Harvey) (2002)

Personal Leadership, Taking Control of Your Work Life (2001)

180 Ways to Walk the Leadership Talk (2000)

HOW GREAT LEADERS GET GREAT RESULTS

JOHN BALDONI

McGraw-Hill

New York   Chicago   San Francisco   Lisbon   London   Madrid   Mexico City
Milan   New Delhi   San Juan   Seoul   Singapore   Sydney   Toronto

The **McGraw·Hill** Companies

Copyright © 2006 by John Baldoni. All rights reserved. Printed in the United States of America. Except as permitted under the United States Copyright Act of 1976, no part of this publication may be reproduced or distributed in any form or by any means, or stored in a data base or retrieval system, without the prior written permission of the publisher.

1 2 3 4 5 6 7 8 9 0   DOC/DOC   0 9 8 7 6 5

ISBN 0-07-146487-5

McGraw-Hill books are available at special quantity discounts to use as premiums and sales promotions, or for use in corporate training programs. For more information, please write to the Director of Special Sales, Professional Publishing, McGraw-Hill, Two Penn Plaza, New York, NY 10121-2298. Or contact your local bookstore.

This book is printed on recycled, acid-free paper containing a minimum of 50% recycled, de-inked fiber.

Library of Congress Cataloging-in-Publication Data

Baldoni, John.
    How great leaders get great results / by John Baldoni.
        p.   cm.
    Includes bibliographical references and index.
    ISBN 0-07-146487-5 (alk. paper)
    1. Executive ability—United States.   2. Leadership—United States.   I. Title.

    HD38.25.U6B35   2005
    658.4'092—dc22

                                                                    2005022881

To my father, L. P. Baldoni, M.D.
Who made so much possible

Contents

Acknowledgments

This book is the result of ideas that were generated in my earlier books about how leaders connect with their people in ways that move their organizations forward in positive directions. Seeking to impose a kind of order on my thinking, I developed a mental model for how leaders use communications. Gradually I realized that communications are central to every step in the leadership process. There is an element of communications in everything that leaders do. For example, an organization needs to know where it should go, and it looks to its leader to provide guidance by setting expectations and seeking input from others. Likewise, when an organization is striving to execute a plan, it is up to its leader not only to provide direction but also to listen to the organization.

And, as with all human endeavors, leadership is not linear. There is risk, and sometimes it requires courage to take those risks. Here, the leader must be front and center by recognizing opportunities as well as demonstrating the bravery to persevere in the face of hardships. The net result of leadership is inspired results. Such results need to be communicated to those inside and outside the organization so that everyone knows what has been accomplished as well as what more needs to be done.

Just as no leader works without the support of others, no management author works in a vacuum. I want to thank Kathy Macdonald and Chuck Dapoz for their early support of this book's concept. Gene Schutt deserves thanks for his keen insight into alignment and results. And, of course, I want to thank the many people who have attended my workshops and keynotes over the years. Their questions and comments have helped shape my ideas.

I also want to thank my agent, Jeff Herman, for seeing the potential of this book. My editor, Donya Dickerson, was once again in my corner. Her professionalism, combined with her support and enthusiasm, is invaluable. Janice Race kept the copy in order, ably supported by copyeditor, Jim Madru. On the home front, my wife, Gail, is my biggest booster. Again, thank you.

PROLOGUE

"Managers are people who do things right
and leaders are people who do the right
thing."[1]

Warren G. Bennis and Burt Nanus
Leaders: Strategies for Taking Charge

*T*HE OLD MAN WAS DYING, AND HE KNEW IT. *But before
he could die, he felt he must tell his story. The
reasons were plenty, but two are prominent.
First, he wanted to put down in his own words what the
war in which he had played such a pivotal role was like
from his perspective as the leading general of his side. As
he wrote his story, he sought advice from a prominent
author. The advice he received was put to good use. He
finished the book just prior to dying. The storyteller was
Ulysses S. Grant, and his adviser was none other than
Mark Twain. The story that Grant told was how one man
of modest circumstance and with limited ambition could
rise to become the general who forced the South to surrender in the bloodiest conflict in American history.
There is nothing in the memoir that dwells on his subsequent presidency—and with good reason; it was not very
successful.*

Grant, of course, had a second reason for writing his memoirs: to earn money for his family. Twain also served as his publisher; Grant himself negotiated a sweet deal. Fortunately, the book was a huge seller and generated for his wife, Julia, a half-million dollars (an enormous sum in the late nineteenth-century). Grant's example of storytelling, therefore, serves a dual purpose—message and results. That lesson is what all leaders can learn—develop your communications to relate a specific point of view in order to achieve intended results. Every day leaders from the top floor to the shop floor, the front lines to the supply lines, and the streets to the plazas do what Grant did: communicate clearly, purposefully, and with style and grace.[2]

What is life if not a story? We are born, a beginning. We grow and develop, a middle. We die, the end. Prosaic to be certain, but a narrative nonetheless. It is no wonder, then, that stories exist all around us in a kind of soup, a rich soup of ideas, myths, opinions, and narrative. If we drink of this soup, we come to an understanding of ourselves as individuals, with obligations to ourselves, our families, and our communities. When our forefathers gathered around the fires, huddled for warmth as well as for protection from fierce creatures, they told stories. Judged by the art they left behind on the walls of caves, and still echoed in song stories of aboriginal peoples, these stories were life lessons on prime concerns—food, shelter, and society.

It is only now, many millennia later, that we have come to rediscover the story for ourselves as a powerful tool for understanding the way our organizations work and how we might use them to achieve our goals. Walk the halls of any company, and you will find images on the walls that speak of achievements of founders as well as employees. Listen to the voices of the people, and you will learn the legacy as well as of the future. Stories abound; they remind us from where we have come, where we are now, and where we are capable of going. Such stories reflect our lives as well as our aspirations. And when stories are told by leaders who want us to succeed, such communiqués provide us with reasons why we must continue to push forward to fulfill our dreams. Lofty perhaps, but isn't that what stories should do? Inspire us to achieve what we are capable of achieving.

HOW GREAT LEADERS GET GREAT RESULTS

How Great Leaders Get Great Results blends management principles and leadership stories framed around the key concept that leaders must communicate with their people in order to make good things happen. The focus of leadership must be to build trust and drive results. In the principles section, we will explore how managers can use stories to explicate their points related to vision, alignment, execution, discipline, risk, and courage. Each chapter will feature a profile of a leader who can articulate the principles through his or her personal example. While most of the leaders may not be considered storytellers in a conventional sense, all the leaders profiled have a good story to tell and communicate leadership through their personal achievements and their leadership examples. As a result, their stories radiate value and truth.

Among those results-driven leaders profiled in the book are

- *Carlos Ghosn*—Brazilian-born CEO of Nissan (now CEO of Renault) who spearheaded the turnaround of the Japanese automaker and in the process helped return it to profitability and respect.

- *Steve Jobs*—founder and CEO of Apple Computer who has served as a visionary leader for the fusion of technology and life and in the process has transformed Apple from a computer company into full-fledged consumer lifestyle company involved in technology, music, and the arts.

- *Anne Mulcahy*—CEO who has helped shepherd the most recent turnaround at Xerox. Mulcahy is a leader who listens well and delegates; she also is a model of work-life balance.

- *Lou Gerstner*—former CEO of IBM who rescued the company by holding it together, building its components into strong business units, and pushing it to focus on new ways to service customers.

- *Bill Belichick*—three-time Super Bowl winning coach of the New England Patriots who has melded superior game strategy with a team ethos that produces healthy results for the team, the owner, and the fans.

- *Jennifer Granholm*—energetic governor of Michigan who has piloted the state nobly through tough economic times with a blend of straight talk and innovative ideas.

- *John McCain*—former POW who spent five and a half years in a North Vietnamese prison camp and now is a U.S. senator known for putting integrity and ethics before political expediency.

- *Meg Whitman*—the CEO who helped eBay become the world's leading consumer auction house and in the process strengthened the brand as well as the organization.

- *Steven Spielberg*—legendary filmmaker whose films are a testament to a creative mind as well as a commitment to stories that make the emotional connection on a personal and societal level.

PRACTICAL AND PROVEN

The combination of leadership principles and stories gives *How Great Leaders Get Great Results* a framework on which managers can learn the importance of story as a tool to enlist support for their ideas and achieve results. This book is a mixture of story and theory framed around a key concept about the purpose of leadership: *Build trust and drive results.*

Through the stories told about people and organizations, you will come to an understanding of the story dynamic as a communications tool to further your leadership aims. *How Great Leaders Get Great Results* will provide practical and proven techniques for how leaders can use stories to bring people together, get them excited about an endeavor, and release their energies on mutual goals. You also will learn to create your own stories and in the process create more "heroes in the workplace"—men and women committed to fulfilling the vision as they improve themselves, their teams, and their organizations. Good stories enhance your leadership results, so good luck, and enjoy the narrative and the results it generates.

"Leadership that lasts is leadership that delivers because that's what feeds credibility. People are willing to go the extra mile, they're willing to work much more, they're willing to sacrifice, but they want some kind of achievement."[1]

Carlos Ghosn
CEO, Renault

WHY LEADERS NEED TO COMMUNICATE

THREE STORIES WITH A PURPOSE

Lying prone, staring at the ceiling, strait-jacketed with medical apparatuses and pain must have given him another hard look at mortality that he had narrowly escaped so often throughout his short life, often as a patient and once as a war hero, but which had claimed his older brother and sister years before. Unable to travel, or even leave his hospital bed, he sought for a way to make a statement about who he was as senator and potential president. His statement emerged not as a speech, a policy paper, nor as an editorial. Rather he chose to tell a story, more precisely six stories, about men facing great moral crises over which they put ambition aside for the greater societal good, often at great personal cost. Together with an aide, he published the stories as Profiles in Courage. *The book was an immediate hit and earned a Pulitzer Prize. The author was John F. Kennedy, assisted by his aide, Ted Sorensen, and the book demonstrated that Kennedy too was a man of conviction, compassion, and yes, even courage.[2]*

A century earlier, another president, exasperated by his general's reluctance to fight, told a story of a monkey who wished for a longer tail. At his every request, the tail grew longer, but still the monkey was not satisfied. Finally, the tail grew so long and heavy that the monkey could not move. The president then eyed his general and said, in effect, and that is where we stand today—too big and fat to fight. The general was George McClelland, and the president was Abraham Lincoln, not only one of our nation's greatest leaders, but also undoubtedly one of our greatest storytellers. It was a habit he learned as a country lawyer to make his points to reluctant juries as well as in the evening entertaining of his fellow lawyers in local inns along the circuit.[3]

Today, there is another kind of story making the rounds. It has been said that in the world of information technology (IT), six months is the average length of any new product or service innovation. After that time, the competition typically has caught up and issued its own product release that may be as good, if not better. The pressure to innovate is relentless; the challenge of continuing to grow can be overwhelming. Somehow Carol Bartz has learned to master both innovation and growth; she's the CEO *of Autodesk, one of the most respected technology companies in the world. From 1992 through 2004, Bartz helped her company grow annual revenues by a factor of three, to just under $1 billion. Her story, and that of her company, is one that is focused on results.*

Autodesk, according to its Web site, is the "world's leading software and services company for the building, manufacturing, infrastructure, digital media, and wireless data fields." According to Bartz, that leadership is a result of understanding customer needs as well as giving credit where credit is due. One of her favorite sayings is, "If God didn't make it, my customers did." From a strategic point of view, decentralization in the hands of consumers is a good thing; it propelled Autodesk to sell software subscriptions—not a unique concept, but one that is recent to her company. Bartz says, "Our idea is to democratize this software for all size companies so they can get productive."[4] Under Bartz, Autodesk has emerged as a global software provider with more than half of all revenues coming from either Europe or Asia. A push into 3D promises even more growth.

Still, Bartz understands that growth does not come from balance sheets; it comes from people—including women, traditionally unrepresented in the technology sector. In an editorial for Autodesk's home town newspaper, the San Jose Mercury News, *Bartz made a strong plea for more women engineers. Lamenting the fact that only 1 in 10 engineers is female, Bartz framed the issue as one that should concern all senior leaders. "No responsible CEO," writes Bartz, "would try to build a business by ignoring the value of half her available capital. That would abrogate her responsibility. . . ." Sadly, that, argues Bartz, is exactly what is happening in the IT world, and as such, it is "irresponsible corporate behavior by failing to take advantage of one-half of the available human 'capital.'" Bartz puts the onus of recruitment on the private sector; competitive wages are not enough. Displaying the savvy of a business leader located in the fastest-moving sector of the global economy, she urges companies to "re-energize [engineering] and re-introduce the 'cool factor' that engineering once possessed."[5]*

Such wisdom always has been associated with Bartz. However, in the late 1990s, Bartz seemed to lose some of her luster; she was criticized for not pursuing dot-com business more aggressively. Her name was omitted from the list of most influential business leaders. No more. In spring 2005, Lee Gomes of the Wall Street Journal *praised her for "sticking to her knitting." That is developing a strategy and sticking with it. As a result, she resumed a familiar position on the list of the world's most influential business leaders.[6] One gets the idea that Bartz does not put much faith in such lists. Her focus is on the bottom line, as well as the future of her industry and the people in it. Not a bad priority for an executive at the helm of a fast-moving industry leader—and one with a good story to tell.[7]*

৶৩ ৩৶

Communication is essential to the leadership process. It is the means of conveyance a leader uses to transmit the inner self to the outer world. Leadership by nature is about pushing people forward. Kennedy and Lincoln both galvanized the spirit of America. As has been said of Lincoln, and can be applied to Kennedy and other great leaders, he spoke to our aspirations. Carol Bartz has pulled her company together and in the process has helped Autodesk become a software industry leader. Such leaders speak to the aspirations of people to do better. They radiate optimism in times of crisis. They provide hope in trying times: Lincoln during the long years of Civil War, Kennedy during the Cold War, and Bartz during the ups and downs of the business cycle. Such men and women lead others from a sense of destiny that comes from acute self-knowledge, as well as a conviction of a better tomorrow. For such leaders, their communications are a means of expressing their authenticity as well as spreading their message.

COMMUNICATION PUSHES RESULTS

Communication is essential for leadership. It is also essential for results. Yet in survey after survey communication always comes out on the short end of the stick. For example, in 2002 and 2004, studies conducted by the *Wall Street Journal* and Harris Interactive surveyed recruiters as to the attributes they were most looking for in MBA job candidates. Communication along with "interpersonal skills" topped the chart.[8] Surveys within companies show a similar need. Everyone cries for more communication, but it seldom appears. You have only to review the results of executives' 360-degree evaluations (assessments based on information gained from superiors, peers, and subordinates) to see that communication is a blind spot. By this we mean that managers believe they are communicating, but they are not. Repeatedly they fail to articulate a message more than once, they fail to listen attentively, and worse, they do not learn. Communication is not a nice to have—it's a *must do.*

One way to elevate the role of communication and give it the urgency it requires is to link it to results. The purpose of leadership is to build trust and achieve results; this is what leaders strive to do for themselves and for their organizations. By linking goals to results, communication can bridge the gap. Specifically, here is what results-oriented communication and stories can do:

- *Define purpose.* As with any message, begin with why! Why are you saying anything? Is it to inform, exhort, or inspire? Or simply to entertain? Winston Churchill told his stories to rally a nation facing calamity from the Third Reich. Likewise, corporate leader Lou Gerstner used his communications to inform people inside and outside of IBM what needed to be done to save the company. Steve Jobs, of Apple, positioned his company as the trailblazer for technology and design as it applies to information and entertainment. Jennifer Granholm, as governor of Michigan, a state facing hard economic times, played it straight with her constituents. She told the truth as she saw it, but she also provided an avenue of hope by offering solutions in the form of initiatives for education, jobs, and enterprise.

- *Showcase people.* The old cliché in journalism is that "people make pictures, and names make news." Both come to life in stories, in particular stories about individual achievements within a company. Tell the story of the customer service rep who went to extraordinary lengths to satisfy a customer. Talk about the engineer who tinkered his way into a new process that improved quality. Speak about the manager who coached an employee to better performance. This approach is something that Meg Whitman of eBay uses when she speaks about eBay's community of users; these are the men and women who make eBay the success that it is.

- *Make the impossible possible.* Stories make the unreal real. If you likened a project at work to climbing a mountain, people would nod unenthusiastically. But if you likened the task to a real-life climb, say, that of Sir Edmund Hillary and Tensig Norgay's trek up Mount Everest, you would get people to tune into your story. If you told of the hardships that Hillary and Norgay shared and the obstacles they overcame through teamwork on their historic journey to "top of the world," you would get people hunching forward really paying attention. And maybe that story would encourage your employees to think of the possibilities of what they might achieve in their own lives. The point of such stories is to inspire. Carlos Ghosn entered Nissan as a complete outsider; few gave him a chance to succeed at this then-floundering automaker. But Ghosn played his ability to connect with people through his communications, giving people confidence that he and his team might be on the right track.

And as coach of the New England Patriots, Bill Belichick has led his team to Super Bowl victories multiple times. For his teams, the toughest challenges become achievable through hard work, dedication, and teamwork, all of which Belichick preaches relentlessly.

- *Reflect organizational character.* Communication must say something about the organization's character. The story must exemplify what the organization cherishes— integrity, ethics, honor, and service are common themes of good stories. Anne Mulcahy defied the odds at Xerox; many wanted her to break the company up and sell it off. Having grown up as a manager at Xerox, Mulcahy relied on the strength of her people to make the existing enterprise succeed. She married the reality of the market to the Xerox culture.

- *Promote courage.* Nothing is easy for very long in business. Leadership is about making decisions that exact a degree of toughness. To lead from the front, you must have courage. John McCain learned the value of courage in a POW camp in North Vietnam; he also practices that courage today as a senator who is not afraid to take positions contrary to his party if he believes they are right for the nation. Two of Steven Spielberg's most powerful films, *Saving Private Ryan* and *Schindler's List,* feature men either in combat or in wartime making courageous decisions to save others from harm's way.

ENABLING LEADERSHIP

Leadership, like a finely crafted story, is an act of persuasion to a point of view that embraces doing good for individuals, teams, and the organization. This is the ideal. The reality is that leadership is persuasion to a point of view that is good for the organization but involves tough choices about teams and individuals. It is up to the leader to make the right call at the right time. Often the choices are difficult and painful. For national leaders, it may mean going to war for self-preservation or negotiating for peace at the risk of further terrorism. For CEOs, it may be closing a plant that employs thousands or keeping the plant open and risking fiscal uncertainty. For managers, it may involve promoting one highly talented individual over another highly talented individual. The need to make difficult decisions occurs with regularity in any job.

Preparation for such decisions is part of the leadership process, so it is useful to understand exactly what leaders do. Specifically, leaders use their communications to do four things that, in turn, drive all the steps of the leadership process.

Aspire. Present the goal by setting
- *Vision*—where the organization is headed
- *Alignment*—how the organization will get there

Perspire. Transform ideals into actions by demanding
- *Execution*—what the organization needs to do
- *Discipline*—how the organization stays the course

Require. Demonstrate creativity and conviction by enabling
- *Risk*—how the organization "rolls the dice" (wisely)
- *Courage*—how individuals keep pushing ahead despite the odds

Transpire. Turn actions into achievements that drive
- *Results*—when goals are fulfilled

When leaders aspire, perspire, and require in order that results may transpire, they are leading from the front. They are pushing their organizations in ways that promote trust. They are helping to drive vision, alignment, execution, and discipline, as well as enabling risk and promoting courage. What holds the leadership process together is regular and consistent communication from the leader. Such leadership communication, enriched through storytelling, becomes the great enabler by which leaders can achieve intended results.

WHY STORIES

Leaders use stories first and foremost to get their points across in a memorable way. If you think about it, we humans have been listening to stories since before the beginning of time. Consider the cave paintings in France, the hieroglyphs in Egypt, and the line drawings in Australia. What are they but stories? The same goes for the *Iliad* and the *Odyssey*. From Homer through Herodotus and on through Chaucer and Shakespeare, we love the telling of a tale. And with a tale, a leader can make a point, not with a proverbial hammer, but with style, deftness, and wit.

A powerful way to communicate a key message is by telling a story. Lincoln used fables and folklore; Kennedy wrote profiles and related anecdotes; Carol Bartz and other business leaders narrate the accomplishments of their employees. Stories are an effective means of placing messages into organizational context. Stories can imbue information with humanity, enabling the communicator to make a connection between the rational and the emotional. In doing so, stories become conduits that make leadership messages meaningful and facilitate intended results.

HOLISTIC LEADERSHIP COMMUNICATION

You can even consider leadership itself as an expression of a story with multiple properties. For example, stories are embedded into the backbone of an organization; they are both the expression and the echo of the culture. Stories are the sinews that bind one group to another; as sinews, they can bend and twist but do not break. Stories also are like muscles—strong, flexible, and powerful. And in another way, stories are like charged particles zinging this way and that throughout the organization with no defined direction. At the same time, stories are the tissues, the organic fabric, that draws people together into a cohesive whole.

Given the complexity of story properties, it is no wonder that communication itself is not an easy task to manage. One reason is that it is not simply a task. For leaders, the task is to inspire and set direction. For managers, the task is to inform and follow up. For followers, the task is to pay attention and provide feedback. For everyone, the task is to listen to one another. The challenge is to embrace all aspects of communication in order to succeed. And one way to do this is to frame communication into leadership stories.

CREATING RESULT-DRIVEN HEROES

Storytelling is a natural communication tool for leaders. An outcome of storytelling is the creation of results-driven heroes, people who have arisen from within the organization to achieve, contribute, and succeed by producing results. Telling these tales in conversations, dialogues, and speeches communicates possibilities; in turn, people become inspired. Now, in the wake of corporate governance scandals, as well as our uneasy economic times, the need for inspiration has never been greater. Rather than looking up, though, it may be wiser to look around. The CEO has fallen off the pedestal; the person who tells the truth and "walks the talk" is the genuine article. Organizations need people of integrity to remain in place and continue to do the work. Organizations also need to put those people in positions where they can manage others and lead by example.

Results-driven heroes come in all shapes, sizes, and guises. You can find them on the shop floor teaching others the job. You can find them in the office suites making the case for customer rights. You can find them in the boardroom arguing for what is good for society rather than expedient for the company. The underlying theme in heroism is integrity—the ability to stand up and be counted. From integrity emerges courage—the willingness to do what is right even at personal cost. And finally, heroism is about putting the needs of other people first. Companies have heroes throughout their ranks; it is a matter of finding them and elevating them as role models.

As logical and aligned as we desire our organizations to be, sometimes the best way to fulfill the vision is to allow people to step out of bounds—not morally, but creatively. Leaders need to create environments where risks are acceptable and encouraged as long as those risks are in line with the mission, culture, and values of the organization. Therefore, stories about risk takers, those who succeeded and those who did not, can do much to enable people to take managed risks for the good of their organizations.

The net outcome of leadership is fulfillment—or results. So much of leadership is focused on achieving objectives—and rightly so—that we sometimes forget to discuss what happens when the vision is fulfilled. From results emerges a kind of joy, the celebration of objectives met, recognition of achievements, and most important, rewards for the contributors. Leadership stories again add to the fulfillment by enabling results to be publicized and people to be recognized as contributors, achievers, and yes, even heroes!

STORIED PATH

Another way to look at leadership is as a journey, a shared experience between leader and follower that occurs over time and space. As such, the journey itself becomes the central story line. There may be dozens and dozens, maybe hundreds of smaller individual stories and anecdotes, but the spine is the push for results. The individual stories are absolutely critical because they imbue the journey with a human dynamic, but the journey from vision to results is the grand heroic story. Noted consultant, author, and editor Nick Morgan writes in his seminal book on public speaking that a good speech can be structured along a single story line.[9] By extension, you can look at the entire leadership journey from vision through results as a single story; it is the push to make the vision reality.

People need communications to point the way, but they need a strong story to give momentum to the journey and many smaller stories to enrich the journey. The story of how Carlos Ghosn and his team helped to turn around Nissan, a company deep in debt and with a declining market share, is inspirational. Ghosn did many things, but most important, he used communication to energize the workforce; he tapped into their collective know-how and made them feel that Nissan's rescue was up to them. Ghosn, like all successful leaders, blends his personal commitment with collective commitment from the organization. The communications of such leaders reinforce vision, alignment, execution, discipline, and results and make the dream come alive. When you add stories about people pulling together, you also provide solace in times of hardship and joy in times of accomplishment.

Stories, particularly those about people engaged in the leadership journey, bond the leader to the follower, as well as followers to one another. In addition, they emphasize the mission—what we are here to do. Stories make the journey human, and when it is human, it leaps from imagination to something that can be done. Ultimately, this is what leadership is all about—achieving inspired results that make the organization a better place for customers, employees, and stakeholders.

Leadership Story Planner: Getting Started

Effective leadership is built on good beginnings. As you consider your leadership journey, reflect upon the following questions. As you write responses, think about stories from within your organization or from something that you have read that might support what you are trying to do.

- *Vision.* Where do you think your organization should go? Why?

- *Alignment.* How will you rally people behind the vision? What will motivate them to follow your vision?

- *Execution.* What needs to be done to achieve the vision? Why will these things be necessary?

- *Discipline.* How will you ensure that people do what is expected of them? How will you reinforce accountability?

- *Risk.* Why will risk be necessary to achieve the vision? How will you encourage people to take risks?

- *Courage.* What can you to do demonstrate courage to your team and to foster it in your teammates?

- *Results.* How will you know when you have arrived? What will be different? What will be better?

Communication Action Steps

- *Aspire.* Tell people where you want to go.
- *Perspire.* Be honest about hardships.
- *Require.* Set clear expectations.
- *Transpire.* Discuss the end results.

CARLOS GHOSN

Perhaps the first thing you might want to know about this person is a story that circulates about him. It says that if he were to sign up with either Ford or General Motors, he could increase their market capitalization by $10 billion. This statement tells you that the executive knows how to get results. He is credited widely for rescuing Nissan from the ash heap of the automobile industry. He is Carlos Ghosn, the brightest star in the automotive industry and now CEO of Renault. What that multi-billion-dollar pen stroke does not tell you is how Ghosn (rhymes with *cone*) does it. Not by wielding a big stick but by connecting with people one on one or one to many. Unlike the industry titans of yore, Carlos Ghosn is a born outsider (born in Brazil of Lebanese parents) who has used his outsider status to observe situations, diagnose problems, and—here's his gift— get people of different backgrounds, cultures, and mind-sets to work together. His legendary status grew at Nissan, but it was born in Brazil.[10]

CROSS-CULTURAL ROOTS

Son of Lebanese immigrants, Ghosn spent his early years in Rio de Janeiro, one of the most cosmopolitan cities in the world. He was educated at a Jesuit prep school in Lebanon and later moved to Paris to study at the elite École Polytechnique, where he earned both undergraduate and master's degrees in engineering. Along the way, he picked up four languages, not counting Japanese. He joined Michelin primarily because of his Brazilian roots, but in the Michelin system, managers with potential start in the factory. It was there that Ghosn, with his ability to assimilate well, learned of the depth of dissatisfaction that exists between hourly and management workers. He was a quick study, and by age 26 he was running a facility of 700 employees in France. Soon he was transferred to Brazil, a famous proving ground for turnaround artists because its businesses periodically swing high and low. Ghosn proved equal to the task and turned the Brazilian operation into a star performer. He was transferred to Michelin North America and again performed well. François Michelin thought so highly of Ghosn that he assigned his son, Eduoard, to work for him. And this was shortly after Eduoard had been named as one of three directors of Michelin. Ghosn also realized that Michelin was a family enterprise and that he would never become a senior leader.[11]

Fortunately, Ghosn's performance caught the eye of Louis Schweitzer, grandnephew of Dr. Albert Schweitzer, the Nobel Laureate, and then CEO of Renault. He named the young man number 2, making Ghosn the first non-French-born executive ever to hold such a senior position at Renault; Ghosn was on track to be his successor. However, there was one little assignment that got in the way. And it was one that Ghosn himself had first suggested to Renault—purchasing a stake in the failing Nissan. While Ghosn himself played a small role in the negotiations, Renault paid $5.4 billion for a controlling stake in the Japanese automaker. Schweitzer knew that he had the perfect candidate to run the enterprise—Ghosn himself.[12]

MOVE TO JAPAN

Now, if there is one thing you have to know about Japanese business, it is that *gaijin* in command are not welcomed kindly. Other than General Douglas MacArthur—who, according to biographer William Manchester, ruled post-World War II Japan as an "American Caesar," thereby setting the country on the course of democracy and reconstruction—few outsiders have held senior executive positions. Japanese businessmen are voracious learners, and they take lessons from all quarters and comers (hence their success in consumer goods manufacturing in terms of quality and performance). However, they are not inclined to see outsiders as worthy of emulation. All this changed

with Carlos Ghosn, though, and as with most things of consequence, it wasn't easy.

Truth be told, even Carlos Ghosn had his doubts. He says
that he was received with "curiosity and skepticism." Moreover,
"I was convinced that as a foreigner coming to Japan, I would
have no chance, zero, of budging the system one inch." Such
resistance is not exclusive to the Japanese; any organization in
crisis will fight to maintain the status quo until things get really
dire. Rather than fight, therefore, Ghosn knew that "Nissan
would have to be changed from the inside."[13] He learned to
speak some Japanese, but he also spoke something that everyone at Nissan understood—the language of business. He and his
team developed plans and metrics and held people accountable.

Most important, Ghosn began with what he calls his "clean
sheet of paper." Jumping into the frying pan, especially one that
is roiling with debt and low morale, requires a deep understanding of people. Ghosn knew the financials, and they were
daunting—declining market share, falling revenues, and $22
billion of debt. He did not know the people, and so, rather than
imposing his system, he spent much of his first 90 days in 1999
getting to know people. According to David Magee in *Turnaround*, Ghosn flew everywhere in the Nissan world, landing at
a facility and then meeting and mingling. He asked questions
and made it known that he wanted the ideas of Nissan employees. This requires tremendous discipline because executives
climb to where they are by imposing order on chaos. In fact, he
was criticized by some in the media for not imposing solutions;
after all, he was the famous *"le cost-killer"* from France who
would save the Nissan day. Ghosn knew better; he wanted to
know what Nissan was capable of doing first.[14]

One thing that Ghosn did immediately was copy an idea he
had developed from his years as a manager in Brazil and later
in the United States—blend cultures. At Nissan, he went one
step further; he created cross-functional teams of employees
from many different disciplines, for example, engineering,
finance, and marketing. Such a mixture gave teams different

perspectives on problems, as well as fresh eyes to suggest solutions. He also sprinkled these teams with a few French people. After putting the cross-functional teams into gear, coupled with getting to know his people, Ghosn launched the Nissan Revival Plan that would cut debt, reduce costs, trim the number of platforms, and begin to restore Nissan to profitability. Ghosn also made a personal commitment: If the plan did not succeed, he and his executive team would resign.[15]

DRIVING EXECUTION

Plans are one thing; implementing them is another. Having been through turnarounds before, Ghosn had the experience to know what to expect. Communication is essential, and Ghosn places high value on it, especially in a cross-cultural environment. Language became an issue. One Renault/Nissan manager noted that meetings would last many times longer because of the simultaneous translation. A solution was proffered: English would be the common language, one not native to either Japanese or French, but the international language of business. However, as prodded by Ghosn, Nissan managers created a dictionary of 40 key business words that everyone would know and understand implicitly. Among them were *focus* and *commitment. Focus* was the narrowing of attention on a specific problem; *commitment* was the "promise" to get it done.[16]

Consistency is essential to a turnaround effort. Setting expectations and following through on them are important to every manager, but they are especially important to a manager broaching from one culture to another. "Consistency in management is something people are expecting in difficult times," says Ghosn. "They like you to be a little predictable." Such consistency "empowers them to make decisions because they know exactly how you are going to react."[17]

Complementing consistency with urgency, in reading accounts of Ghosn by others as well as in reading his own words, the need to move quickly appears again and again. However, speed at the top is different from speed at the bottom. This is why Ghosn made certain that such urgency was communicated clearly and repeatedly. One way you drive speed is to empower managers. This was a radical concept in Japan at the time; managers at first were hesitant. The French team had its doubts, but the Japanese managers quickly proved their mettle and made decisions, executed them, and eventually delivered.[18]

Nissan did have to make cuts in the labor force, some 21,000 workers in all. Speaking a few years later, Akira Takahura, a Nissan union leader, recalls Ghosn being sensitive to worker needs at the Murayama plant that was closed. To avoid layoffs, workers had three choices: relocation, voluntary retirement, or traveling to another plant away from their families. For those who chose the latter, Nissan provided three paid trips home per month, two more than is typical. Takahura also points out that of the 21,000 jobs Nissan eliminated company-wide, none were layoffs; reductions were made via attrition or voluntary retirement.[19]

The Nissan Revival Plan was an ambitious plan that was originally slated to take three years. The miracle is that it required one year less to achieve results. Ghosn then was named CEO; he had begun his tenure as chief operating officer; the president and CEO had remained a Japanese national in deference to its management culture. Within two years, Nissan had more than halved its debt and was well on the road to profitability, achieving record earnings. In just two years, Nissan had gone from losses of $5.7 billion to gains of nearly $3 billion for fiscal year 2001. Ghosn announced in 2002 that the Nissan Revival Plan was "over" and with appropriate deference attributed its success to its employees.[20]

More important for the future, Ghosn had launched new vehicles successfully and had more new products in the pipeline. Every CEO knows that you cannot cost-cut your way to profitability over the long term. Nissan had rediscovered its product magic. The all-new Altima was named "Car of the

Year" at the 2002 North American International Auto Show. Soon enough the new G35 rolled out to strong reviews and, even better, strong sales. Design always was a strong hallmark at Nissan; for Nissan, design was wholly cross-cultural, a blend of designers working at corporate headquarters in Japan as well as at the famed Nissan Center International studio in San Diego, California. Shiro Nakamura was recruited from Isuzu to head Nissan's design team. Under Nakamura's leadership—and at Ghosn's insistence—"an important driving force of Nissan [was] design." Ghosn knew that automotive design drives brand and, in turn, brings people to the showrooms because they want to see what is new, different, and exciting.[21]

Success at Nissan made Ghosn everything from the hero of a *manga*, a form of Japanese comic book series, to a business icon who was named *Fortune* magazine's "Asia 2002 Business-man of the Year." In addition, Ghosn was selected by *Automotive News* as "Industry Leader of the Year" and "Top CEO—Asia" in 2001 and the latter again in 2002. He also wrote a best-seller in Japan. Success, however, has not gone to his head; he has focused on the future. After completion of the Nissan Revival Plan, Ghosn and his team formulated another one in April 2002, Nissan 180. It stands for 1 million more sales by the end of fiscal year 2004, 8 percent return on investment, and zero "net automotive debt." Needless to say, it, too, was accomplished.[22]

CULTURE OF OPPORTUNITY

For Ghosn, the turnaround was all about creating a culture of success. As he says in his own book, *Shift: Inside Nissan's Historic Revival*, it was not Renault's "intention . . . to change Nissan's culture." Change was dictated by circumstance. In Nissan's case, chaos was more the order of the day; management had devolved into a "not my problem" mentality. People were unclear about goals. Profit was an abstract. Ghosn and his team changed that by creating a culture of expectation and holding people accountable. Ghosn believes in management's responsibility to develop future leaders. "Tomorrow's leaders," he writes, "get their training by dealing with today's challenges." In this way, Ghosn states, "you achieve two ends: one, problems are solved; two, managers learn by 'experience.'" Results are what matter most. Japanese managers are noted for long hours; it's called *presence*. However, as Ghosn points out, being present and being productive are not one and the same. Getting things done the right way is what matters most. In return, organizations must be loyal to their people and provide them with opportunities to grow and be rewarded. Bottom line: Ghosn was able to drive change because, as he writes, Nissan had "no other choice" but "rapid return to better results," and "Japan was ready for a revolution."[23]

Ghosn holds himself as CEO most accountable. "The first social responsibility of a CEO is to be the leader of the company." Ghosn sees it as his job to communicate clearly to everyone, not simply the senior leaders. Ghosn said that he spent more time in his early days at Nissan with front-line employees rather than on the upper floors; it was essential that he begin from the ground up, literally and metaphorically. The CEO also must ensure that people know what they are supposed to do; "my vision of the company is continuous," with everyone as individuals and teams pulling weight equally. Rewards will be forthcoming not simply in "bigger paychecks" but also in opportunities for advancement. It is also management's responsibility to improve the conditions of work for employees; improved ergonomics is essential. Finally, the CEO, according to Ghosn, serves as chief strategist, balancing long- and short-term goals, along with clarity and aspiration. You want to keep people enthused and excited about the future.[24]

Ghosn knows what it means to be an outsider. "I've always felt different. . . . [You] try to integrate, and that pushes you to try to understand the environment." This perspective gives him keen insight into the human condition. For example, one former Nissan executive recalls an incident in which a Renault executive chewed out a group of Japanese executives and sent them packing. Ghosn reacted quickly. "Find them and apologize," the Nissan man recalls him saying. "You don't do that in Japan—some of them might jump out of a window."[25]

Ghosn has a delightful sense of humor; it is one of the secrets of his charm. He was voted the second "most desirous husband" in Japan behind a baseball player. This is unheard of for a businessman, let alone a foreign businessman. Some women wanted to marry him. Ghosn, married with four children, imagines telling his grandchildren, "If they tell you you're ugly and unpleasant, you tell them, 'I'm sorry, but this survey shows that a lot of people would have liked to have spent a lot of time with you, some of them all of their lives.'"[26] What's more, he says, his children enjoyed his celebrity status in Japan to a point; when they asked for a life-size poster of him that had been printed in conjunction with the publication of his bestselling book in Japan, *Renaissance*, he provided it, only to find it a short time later "in the trash." A man who will quote that story knows the value of humility.[27]

Ghosn would need plenty of humility for his next assignment—becoming CEO of Renault. In France, CEOs are not celebrities; those who stand out from the pack are not heroes; they are targets. French unions are notoriously tough bargainers. "We're afraid he thinks it's normal to cut heads," said one French union representative. Another union official told the *Wall Street Journal* that Ghosn could expect a "violent reaction" to proposed plant closings or job reductions. Fortunately, Renault in 2005 is in much better shape than Nissan was in 1999. However, analysts are expecting Ghosn to exact changes. Renault's operating margin is less than 6 percent, four points behind Nissan's 10 percent. Just prior to taking over in May 2005, Ghosn repeated a strategy that has worked for him in the past: "I'm starting the job with a clean sheet of paper. I'm not going in with any preconceived ideas."[28]

DOING IT THE RIGHT WAY

Now, as the head of two automakers simultaneously, a feat never before accomplished, Ghosn is a perpetual globetrotter, basing himself in Paris but spending time in Japan as well as in the United States. "[N]ationality is not the determining factor in success. The key is results."[29] Well said by a leader who knows how to get things done but also knows that there is always more to do. The automotive business "is an industry in which comebacks occur rapidly and downfalls occur fast. Managers have to be extremely attentive to changes. . . . [And] if managers get it wrong, the consequences are terrible for the company." He takes this view personally, too. "When you have a good moment, it's good to remember the bad moments, because that will keep your feet on the ground. And when you have bad moments, it's good to remember the good moments, because that helps you keep your head above water."[30]

The good news about Carlos Ghosn, and why he is so widely cheered not only in the business press but also among employees, is that he has achieved his results the right way, that is, *with* people, not in spite of them. Many executives say this but act differently. Ghosn walks the talk—in five different languages, including Japanese, and in three different cultures. Perhaps it is his immigrant background, but more likely it is his commitment to achieving success the only way possible— together with others. His story is one of possibility that is confirmed by results.

Leadership Lessons

- *Be visible*. When Carlos Ghosn took over the reins at Nissan, he made an extraordinary effort to be seen and heard.

- *Listen to your people.* Leadership requires getting to know the organization. Ghosn spent months asking questions and seeking answers from Nissan's own workforce.
- *Leverage your strengths.* Nissan owes its revival to the cross-functional teams; by spreading talent and skills around the organization, everyone benefits from strong ideas as well as new perspectives.
- *Promote your own people.* The success of any organization often comes from within. Ghosn gives credit for the turnaround to the people of Nissan. The company promotes from within, too.
- *Respect others.* Japan is a culture that reveres tradition. Ghosn respected the tradition as he nudged Nissan forward—at warp speed. But such change could only be sanctioned from within by respecting the rights and abilities of employees.
- *Make the impossible possible.* Few people gave Carlos Ghosn much chance at succeeding in Japan; the odds in terms of business and culture were stacked against him. Ghosn tried and succeeded by focusing on people and getting them to commit to results.

Aspire

- *Vision—where the organization is headed*
- *Alignment—how the organization will get there*

*P*eople want to belong to something larger than themselves. They want to contribute to an organization that, as Abraham Lincoln said, "appeals to their better nature." It is the role of the leader therefore to articulate where the organization is going and how it will stay on track while it moves forward.

C H A P T E R

> "We live in an era when more and more of our activities depend on technology. . . . Apple's core strength is to bring very high technology to mere mortals in a way that surprises and delights them and that they can figure out how to use."[1]
>
> *Steve Jobs*
> *CEO, Apple Computer*

VISION

HEROIC VISIONS

They were founded by an ex-military officer, and their hierarchy still uses the term general. *Their vows are strict, but their commitments are even stricter. They are known for their forthright opinions and have on more than one occasion been excommunicated en masse. Their values are love, humility, and service. Their vision is to teach and to serve, and they have been doing that for nearly four centuries. They are the Jesuits, founded by Ignatius Loyola in the sixteenth century in Spain.*

Today, Jesuits are found in every race in every corner of the globe. You will find them in universities, in governments, in hospitals, and even in parishes. The Jesuits are an active order whose mission of service can be fulfilled by many different disciplines. They are first and foremost known as educators; there are a number of Jesuit universities in the world, including the preeminent one, Georgetown, located in Washington, D.C.

Every religious community of any religion—Christian, Islamic, Buddhist, or Jewish—has its salient features of adherence to strict codes. For many communities, the codes are manifest in dress, customs, and culture. Here is where the Jesuits differ. Some Jesuits live in communities with other Jesuits; others live in the civilian world or in parishes. What unites them is a commitment to God and to the order. Their vision is at once open-ended—service to God through others—their mission can be personal and individualized. You will find a Jesuit in just about any kind of profession from farming to medicine, with a healthy dose of academe in between. It is not easy to become a Jesuit; one cannot even begin the process until one graduates from university, and it takes 12 years from there. All those years are not spent in religious training but rather mixed in with graduate-level education and theology and community service work. Thirty-three, the age of Jesus when he died, is a typical age of ordination. (There are many Jesuit brothers who do not become ordained but who hold equally important tasks in the community.)

Perhaps one of their own, Baltasar Gracián, a seventeenth-century Jesuit priest and something of a visionary management thinker, best expressed the concept of aspiration when he spoke of greatness:

Great men are part of their times. It is not everyone who finds the century he deserves. . . . Some men have been worthy of a better century. . . . The truly learned man has one advantage: he is immortal. If this is not his century, many centuries to follow will be.

Well put for an order that has stood the test of time and in the process set forth a vision of service and fulfilled it.[2]

❧ ☙

Few actors who portray heroic figures on the screen ever match that heroism in their off-screen lives. An exception would be Christopher Reeve. At six-foot four, muscular, and handsome, he was an ideal choice to play Superman on screen, but it may have been his portrayal of the superhero's alter ego, Clark Kent, that revealed the real Reeve—vulnerable, humorous, and dedicated to his job. He then defined heroism as "Someone who commits a courageous act without considering the consequences."[3] A graduate of Julliard, Reeve was an accomplished actor who moved easily between theater and film. And after the success of Superman and its three sequels, Reeve used his fame and star power to do a variety of challenging roles, which, as he said, were examples of "escape from the cape."

But it was a horseback riding accident in May 1995 that turned him into a quadriplegic and transformed him into a champion for the dignity and rights of the paralyzed. Reeve's own injuries left him wholly incapacitated from the neck down, breathing only with the help of a ventilator. He did contemplate suicide, but he said that the looks on the faces of his children dissuaded him. Always an avid participant in sports, ranging from skiing and sailing to horseback riding, Reeve applied that competitive spirit to his own rehabilitation. While the injury to his spinal cord was severe, some nerves remained alive, and he worked out vigorously to stimulate the nerves and keep his muscles toned. His workouts *were grueling, but it was a price that he was willing to endure in order to keep himself and his cause alive. This became his heroic vision.*

Despite being confined to a wheelchair, he was an active public figure. He lobbied Congress, and he addressed the Democratic National Convention in 1996. As he told Psychology Today *in 2003, "You have to take action and stand up for yourself— even if you're sitting in a wheelchair." The week before his death in October 2004, he had traveled to Chicago for an event recognizing his efforts, but one among his very public postaccident life that he used to lobby public opinion for further research, including the use of stem cells to regenerate nerve cells.*

He also was active in raising funds for spinal cord research. At the time of his death, The Christopher Reeve Paralysis Foundation had generated more than $46.5 million for continued research. "He became a real-life Superman," said Colin Blakemore, the CEO of Britain's Medical Research Council. "His courage, his heroism was extraordinary." Paul Smith of the Spinal Injuries Association in England said, "He has been our champion. If you think of spinal injuries, you automatically conjure up an image of Christopher Reeve." His example made a positive difference. "He pushed the boundaries as far as he could get them to go," added Smith. "I don't think we could have gotten to where we are now without him."[4]

Even after his injury and resulting paralysis, Reeve continued to act and direct. His most memorable role may have been in a remake of Rear Window, *about a photographer confined to a wheelchair who witnesses a murder. He also directed it, with a special emphasis on close-ups, using his facial expressions, coupled with his dialogue, to tell the story of a person fighting against the confines of his broken body to bring a murderer to justice. Reeve continued working until the end, with his final movie,* The Brooke Ellison Story, *about a young girl paralyzed at age 11 who persevered over paralysis to graduate from Harvard.*

Reeve was always a realist. He confessed that he woke up in the mornings crying, and he stopped workouts on the tread-

*mill and bicycle because he was not making the progress he had
expected. He also changed his definition of heroism to what*
The Economist *paraphrased as "simply enduring."*[5] *Shortly
before his death, he told interviewer Oprah Winfrey that he
expected to walk again. When she asked what would happen if
he didn't, he replied, "Then I won't walk again." Reeve never
again walked, but he took giant strides in pushing for research
and therapies for paralysis and used his talents on screen and
off to demonstrate that courage is not reserved for the able-bod-
ied but can be manifest in all of us. It is what is inside that matters most, and when it came to Christopher Reeve, his courage
was, well, superheroic. His vision continues, and somewhere
Superman must be smiling.*[6]

ശ്ര ൭൭

It is the leader's job to point the organization in the right direction. How leaders do this makes the difference between success
and failure. For the Jesuits, vision represents building universities, helping those in need, and participating in law, science,
and medicine. For Christopher Reeve, the vision was both personal and collective: His striving to become physically able
enabled others to do the same and allowed him to raise funds
for this worthy cause. Always it falls to the leader to paint the
picture of the city in bold relief so that people will want to
aspire to reach it.

Vision, therefore, is the starting point, and as the starting
point, it is necessary to push the organization to look outside
itself to see not what it is now but rather what it can become.
When you think about it, vision is about creating expectations. It
is human nature to be receptive to messages about what might
occur. For example, when Bill Gates announced on December 7,
1995 that Microsoft would focus on the Internet, he set forth the
vision of Microsoft becoming more than it was. While Microsoft
had been hugely successful to date, Gates believed that an even
greater future lay by embracing the Internet. Today, more than a

decade later, Microsoft is going head to head with Google for a place in digital searches that will bring the power of the Internet revolution in data and commerce to the desktop. Better yet, Gates' prodding has meant that Microsoft has avoided organizational apathy that sometimes is the by-product of success.

BALANCING SIMPLICITY AND GRANDEUR

Visions by nature are grandiose. They are meant to uplift people—to carry them away to another place. As you say the words, inspirational anthems may rise up from the echoes of your subconscious. Wonderful! If the vision is to move from imagination to reality, however, it must be simply and directly stated. For example, "Our goal is to become the leading producer of IT systems for the health care business" or "We will become the leading provider of therapies for renal care patients." Each of these statements is direct as well as limited, for example, IT systems for health care, therapies for renal care. Employees can read and absorb them at a glance and later begin to incorporate them.

Simplicity is the beginning. When contemplating the vision, the leader must consider the following points:

- *Think big.* Simplicity of expression does not negate bigness. The most often quoted vision statement is John F. Kennedy's challenge to send a man to the moon and bring him back by the end of the decade. This is straightforward to state, but it involved the efforts of thousands of highly committed people, the development of whole new infrastructures, and the investment of billions to bring to fruition. Likewise, Bill Clinton's desire to provide health care to all Americans, to insure the uninsured, was simple but vague, and while noble, it did not contain the galvanizing spirit to enact. Furthermore, Clinton developed the plan within his administration without asking for the input of Congress, whose task it was to pass it. As a result, without any sense of ownership, the initiative languished, a victim of partisan bickering.[7] Most important, as stated earlier, visions are designed to get people to think beyond the here and now, to envision the potential, and even better, to begin to consider their role in this vision. Thinking big is essential to the success of any vision. In this regard, Steve Jobs is an acknowledged master of painting the big picture. His communications, whether to journalists or to an assembled hall of the Apple faithful, brim with the potential of a future delivered by Apple products, be they PCs or iPods.

- *Focus the vision.* As big and as broad as visions must be, it is up to the leader to keep them focused. A Greek aphorism popularized first by Isaiah Berlin and adapted later by author/consultant Jim Collins says, "The fox knows many things; the hedgehog knows one big thing."[8] Narrowing the vision to one big idea enables the leader to embrace it, but more important, it allows the followers to focus on it. Successful focus on the vision permits better alignment and execution and, ultimately, attainable and achievable results.

- *Describe the vision in real terms.* As grand as the vision may be, it must be made real to the listener. The best way to do this is to tell what the fulfilled vision will be like when achieved. An organization that wants to become a leader in its field must describe what fulfillment will be like. For example, our products will work better than predicted. Customers will become advocates. Journalists will want to do stories on us. Recruiters will want to hire our people. Our stock will be considered an excellent buy and a long-term hold. These are concrete terms that describe what leadership in the field means, and they give momentum to the aspiration. Keep in mind that these aspirations are not strategic (that emerges later in alignment), but they are specific and therefore achievable.

Visions imply the "what's in it for me." In other words, when we achieve our vision, our organization will be a better place for all stakeholders. People will want to come to work because the compensation and benefits are good and the work is rewarding. Customers will want to buy our products or services because they add enrichment to their lives. Shareholders will want to own our stock because of the healthy return.

- *Sell the vision.* Leadership is an act of persuasion. A vision untold is a vision unsold. It is essential to bring people into the tent to see what is happening. Good politicians of any party excel at persuading people to consider their message. Likewise, effective heads of social service agencies or nonprofits do a good job of fundraising because they touch people with the concept of what their organization does. They are selling. And every vision needs a good salesperson—one who is not afraid to be overt in his enthusiasm and consistent in his stories.

- *Communicate the vision in personal terms.* Communication demands involvement. Ask people what you want them to do. Visions are really calls to action; they are the siren calls for engagement. For this reason, visions must embrace people. Phil Knight built Nike by involving employees in every aspect of the business. His communications radiated his commitment. As a result, stories of Knight's commitment and participation in work are legion throughout the company. While the vision statement itself is not a to do list, the stories the leader weaves around it make it clear that employees must participate. The vision must move from what the leader wants to what the people can make happen. The vision, therefore, becomes shared.

All these points—from thinking big to focusing, gut checking, selling, and personalizing—combine synergistically to stimulate the leader to look beyond the horizon, where leaders traditionally have always looked

CREATING THE SHARED VISION

Vision must link the mission. Confusion arises around the difference between vision and mission. Vision is where you want to go. Mission is what you do on the way. (More on mission in Chapter 3.) Inclusion is essential. Otherwise, the vision remains locked within the leader's capabilities and limited to what she and only she can accomplish. When the leader opens up the process to others, everyone has the opportunity to join in. There are many ways to include people. Here are some suggestions:

- *Hold vision off-sites.* Get people together to discuss the vision. Off-site locations work best because they minimize interruptions. Also, if possible, take a cue from what designers do. They "dress" the environment with visual cues consisting of objects to inspire thought. These visual cues can be photographs, works of art, swatches of fabric, or gadgets. By dressing the room, you prepare people to step outside themselves and focus on something different. Along this line, many facilitators who work in vision groups stage activities, games, and even simulations to spark thought. Participation in the vision process is essential.

- *Create vision maps.* Pictures enable people to understand what words cannot express. Invite people to work in teams to create a vision map that involves what they wish to accomplish, what obstacles stand in the way, and what they must do to overcome them. By working in pictures, a visual language, people may feel freer to express a thought or emotion that they might not want to express in words. Icons free people to do this. (*Hint:* If people feel "drawing challenged," provide magazines so that people can cut out pictures to represent their ideas.)

- *Tell vision stories.* Make the journey along the way real. Think of the pioneers who kept diaries as they crossed the land to the territories of Oregon and California. They told stories about what they saw, heard, and even feared. They marked their stories with milestones such as rivers forded, game slaughtered, Indians met (or, sadly, fought), and interesting people along the way. In the same way, people can tell stories about their journeys along the vision trail. Invite people to share stories of their progress. Post the stories on a Web site. Repeat them frequently.

LOCAL VISION

Thus far our discussion of visions has focused on the entire organization. It would be a mistake to think that the vision process is reserved for only leaders of thousands. Vision is necessary to departments, teams, and even individuals. In fact, another word for vision is *direction*. We all need to go where we are headed. Thinking big, focus, description, salesmanship, and aspiration are all integral to *local vision,* that is, vision for the team or the individual.

The local vision also plays a key role in support of the vision for the whole. It is up to the leader of the organization, as well as the team leader, to allow people to buy into it. It is not enough to present it. Followers must make it their own. Part of the buy-in is alignment, which I will describe in the next chapter, but it is also part of the vision process in that the leader must be open and willing to have people *share* in the process. How? By presenting the vision story in terms that involve the participants. Present the story as part of an ongoing process that will never succeed without the support and participation of others. If a CEO stands up and states that he wants the company to be perceived as the best in its category, that's a platitude. If he states that he wants the company to be the best in quality, service, and sales and presents a plan to achieve it, then it becomes a vision.

Part of sharing the vision means creating one for your own department. You must align yourself with it. If your organization does not have a vision, then create one so that you are in alignment with organizational intent, that is, whatever your company does. For example, if you are the chief information officer of a manufacturing concern that makes medical devices, your vision is to put information technology (IT) in support of that enterprise. You and your people should create a vision that supports the functions of the company, for example, research and development, operations, human resources, marketing, sales, and customer service. Your vision is complementary to the company's intention.

As the leader, you need to iterate the vision in your regular communications with people. Whenever you give a presentation or make a report, link the vision to what you are doing. This demonstrates alignment but also gives your people a sense of purpose. The practice may strike some as rigid, but actually, it is merely good discipline. When people are thinking and articulating the vision, they will be creating and working to support it. This is how things get done on time and on budget.

SHAPING COMMUNICATIONS

Vision plays a role in shaping day-to-day communications. When you know what your company stands for, you can better bring your people along with you. You can work cooperatively to set performance expectations and follow up on them with the knowledge that what you are doing is in support of the company. Here are some things to consider when communicating the vision:

- *Proclaim the vision.* Make a big deal of the announcement. Stage an all-employee meeting. Create a pledge wall where people can sign their names to the vision statement; their signature is a symbol of their support.

- *Merchandise the vision.* Tie the vision statement to your corporate logo graphically. Print it on banners and posters and even hats and T-shirts. You want people to know what you stand for.

- *Personalize the vision.* Establish a vision page on the Web site. Invite employees to comment on the vision and what it means to them. Such personalization leads people to do more than support it with words; it will lead them to commit to the vision with actions.

RE-ENVISION

Vision statements, particularly those for departments rather than entire organizations, are not written in clay; they may be altered or replaced with new ones to reflect changing conditions, such as entry into a new market or fulfillment of the vision itself. If you have done what you have set out to do, challenge your people with a new statement of purpose. For example, if the vision for your department was to integrate a new system, and that has been accomplished, you need to think of something else to aspire to.

Departmental visions can play another important role—selling up. If you want the senior leadership team to support you in your efforts, you need to give them reasons why. A good statement of purpose, backed by your vision that complements the organization's vision, is a strong platform on which to build. Vision alone will not prevail, but if it is supported with a well-developed business case, it might tip the balance in your favor. Integration of the vision into communications of all kinds then becomes essential to driving the message home.

SIGN OF COMMITMENT

As a final statement, many organizations ask people to sign the vision statement, or vision map, much like the Founding Fathers put their signatures on the Declaration of Independence. The physical act of signing becomes a tangible sign of commitment. It signifies that the individual cares and will do what is possible to make the vision real. Vision is the lodestone of the organization. It is the leader's responsibility to point the stone in the right direction and ensure that people agree with its direction. The process is never easy, but with constant communication and frequent stories, the vision begins to take on a life of its own.

Vision Story Planner

Visions are about possibilities. Consider what your organization is now and what it can become. Think of stories that will support the following questions:

- What will it take to get people to aspire to a new vision?
- What will they need to acquire to achieve the vision?
- What will you require them to do to achieve the vision?
- How will you keep them motivated to achieve the vision?

Communication Action Steps (Vision)

- *Aspire.* Generate excitement.
- *Perspire.* Focus on what needs to be done.
- *Require.* Remind people what they need to do.
- *Transpire.* Keep communicating, selling, persuading.

STEVE JOBS

The computer screen image said it all: *"Hello!"* It was written in script, and it was featured in an introductory television spot of the Macintosh computer. In 1984, when Mac hit the streets, computers were still considered clunky; the PC revolution was in full stride, but machines were stodgy, screens were green or amber, and software was burdensome. More than 20 years later, Mac has morphed into a fully formed product line from high-end graphic generators to slim, tantalizing notebooks. There's even a mini version. Along the way, though, the man behind the company that builds Macs has morphed himself from ex-CEO into CEO of two trend-setting companies, Apple and Pixar. Along the way, he also has straddled technology and entertainment and, as a result, has legitimized the downloading of songs with not only a licensing agreement with iTunes Music Store but also a whole new way to play those songs on iPods.

Many entrepreneurs are serial creators; they build a business once and then do it again with another business. Some become wealthy but are little known outside the circles of their own industries. Steve Jobs, on the other hand, is an entrepreneur who powered the PC revolution nearly 30 years ago but who has not stopped pushing the envelope with ideas that fuse dreams to reality courtesy of technology. His is a story of drive and ambition but mostly one of a pure and simple vision. Along that quest, he has never stopped telling us where he has been or where he wants to go. He is a consummate storyteller.

All of what Jobs does professionally works on a continuum. As he says, "Pixar is the most technically advanced creative company; Apple is the most creatively advanced technology company." Apple operates from a single premise that Jobs phrases as a question: "How easy is this going to be for the user? How great is this going to be for the user?" Pixar focuses on delivering a story that people will embrace. And it's worked pretty well from *Toy Story* through *Finding Nemo* and later to *The Incredibles*.[9] Such focus has paid off on the bottom line. Revenues at Apple are expected to top $13 billion in 2005. iTunes has a market share of upwards of 70 percent of all downloaded music. *Finding Nemo* was the highest-grossing animated motion picture of all time.

LIVING THE DREAM

First things first. Apple Computer is a classic Silicon Valley enterprise—a couple of guys in a garage really did build a computer whose maturation from toy to billion dollar business not only changed the way the valley works but also changed the way people in the workplace do what they do—and a whole lot more. If you have any doubts, Jobs will be happy to tell you about it. He is not shy. And while his brashness may rub some the wrong way, what he has done, and continues to do, is proselytize for newer and better ways to use technology to accomplish what it is we want to do.

He is in short a gadfly for "what's next." Jobs can back up his boasts with successes—Apple II, the Macintosh, iMac, iPod, and iTunes. And like other entrepreneurs, he has known defeat; a corporate executive he had hired booted him out of his own company. His subsequent computer venture didn't exactly light up the world. And when he did return in triumph to Apple, he had to beg an old nemesis, Bill Gates—the other father of desktop computing—for cash to keep his old company going.

That was only a first step. He pruned products and then introduced a new product, the iMac, that charmed the industry and gained Apple a larger user base. In the meantime, Apple pushed to launch a new operating system based on Unix. It was called Mac OS X. It was called a "moon shot" inside Apple for its bold leap of technology, not to mention its bet on the future. Brent Schlender, who covers Apple for *Fortune,* called OS X a "cross between a Porsche and an Abrams tank." It was as robust as it was elegant and gorgeous to look at. When other developers would not come to play, that is, create applications for this operating system, Apple, true to its heritage, went it alone. And in 2005, the newest version, code named "Tiger," was launched with an even bolder software package, one blending productivity software such as word processing and presentations with lifestyle applications for music and movie editing. Bill Joy, former technology chief of Sun Microsystems and today a bold and insightful philosopher, says, "Everyone in every corner of the software business could learn a lot from iLife." Praise does not come any higher than this.[10]

COMMUNICATIONS EXEMPLAR

What Jobs is today—and has been since he started Apple—is an exemplar of leadership communications. He knows how to use his words, his deeds, and his image—not simply to serve himself—to further the cause of his vision. In short, he knows how to play the public relations game. And lest you be tempted to think that all PR is the same, an examination of how Jobs works is in order.

Pick a moment at Macworld, his company's regular series of user-group trade fairs where the movers and shakers—along with the gremlins of the industry, those who make it work— visit for a couple of days of schmoozing, wheeling and dealing, and one-upmanship. Also in attendance are the media—not simply computer trade journalists but also mainstream and business-stream journalists—along with the financial media— to see what's new and next. Here is where Steve Jobs excels.

He has turned product launches from corporate theater into media events. Alone on the stage, his voice projected by a wireless mike, with a larger-than-life televised image shining above, Jobs has the proverbial computer world in his hand. At these product launches he accomplishes three aims at once: giving the media some news they can play with, reassuring the Apple faithful as well as newcomers to iPod and iTunes that his company will continue to pioneer the frontiers of applied technology, and very important, sending a message back to Cupertino, Apple's headquarters, that Apple is what it has always been— the standard bearer for the PC revolution. Wow! All that in one presentation!

FRAMING THE VISION

Jobs is relentlessly direct about his vision: "We're building the best personal computers that anyone has ever built." He draws distinctions with his competition, concerned only with the financial side of the business. He once disparaged them as "distributors" who all use the same software (Microsoft) and the same components (Intel).[11] By drawing this distinction, Jobs can position Apple as the one true visionary computer maker. His "us versus them" theme plays well to the Apple faithful in Cupertino, as well as to the millions of Apple users.

More recently, however, a change has occurred. There is a three story billboard in the Apple lobby—it is of the iPod. And with good reason. iPod has enabled Apple to merge its edge for technology into an engine for earnings in ways that its computer lineup has never been able to do. Apple accounts for 5 percent of PCs. By contrast, iTunes Music Store accounts for some 70 percent of all music downloads. iPod itself is a megaseller (4.6 million sold in 2004), and its flash-drive version, retailing for as low as $99, has been a big hit, too.

A MELLOWING

Once upon a time, Steve Jobs also was known by his "dark side." Articles about Jobs featured descriptors such as "mercurial," "volcanic," "temperamental," and "paranoid." In 2005, some of the less appealing side reared its head with the publication of an unauthorized biography. Known to be fiercely protective of his private life, Jobs objected. Apple then promptly yanked all books by the book's publisher from its shelves. Perhaps, however, as *The Economist* conjectured, it was all part of an act to stoke the air of mystery that cloaks him and only adds to his legacy.[12] This said, there are more important signs that his leadership skills are improving. As a sign of an "older and wiser" Steve Jobs, he is looking to the next generation and wants to be known as a "recruiter and manager of talent." He has hired a strong team of business executives to surround him with financial and manufacturing expertise. He also has beefed up the board of directors with significant players from Silicon Valley— Larry Ellison of Oracle, Bill Campbell of Intuit, and Art Levinson of Genentech.[13]

In 2004, Jobs was diagnosed with pancreatic cancer. Normally lethal within a matter of months, the type afflicting Jobs is unusual, and with the surgical treatment he received, his 5-year survival rate approaches 90 percent. The next year, 2005, saw Jobs turn 50. He says now that he's feeling fine. Characteristic of Jobs, though, his age presents a unique challenge. "It makes us look further ahead, but it doesn't make us more patient." Still his age has given him perspective. "You know better what questions to ask." Finding the right people for the job also can add time to a project, forcing Jobs to reflect that "we chew on things for a while before we have the A-team go after something."[14]

SPEAKING OUT

As might be expected of a visionary, Jobs is not one to back down from a fight, even when it is with a company with whom he is doing business. The movie industry and the technology hardware companies have been skirmishing over the piracy of online content, be it music or movies. Michael Eisner, chairman of Disney, which held an exclusive distribution contract with Pixar, assailed the technology companies for not doing enough to stop online video piracy. In fact, Eisner even cited Apple's campaign "Rip. Mix. Burn" as an inducement. Jobs, undeterred by the fact that Pixar pictures had earned over $600 million through Disney, was not deferential. Jobs criticized Eisner for misunderstanding the technology; the Apple campaign refers not to online downloading and copying but rather to disc-to-disc copying, which generally is considered legal.[15] "This is an important issue, and it is not going to be solved by threatening rhetoric." Ever the "techoevangelist," Jobs continues: "It's going to be solved by a computer scientist who has an incredibly original idea. We just don't know who or when."[16]

iTunes Music proved to be the answer that many people were looking for. Stepping into the fray created by music swapping, and after the courts declared Napster illegal, Jobs offered a solution: Consumers could buy songs one at a time for 99 cents. The music moguls preferred a license deal, but Jobs, ever the salesman, persuaded them that people do not want to rent music; they want to own it. iTunes Music Store has generated billions in revenue and legitimized downloading. By January 2005, iTunes had sold some 250 million songs. For Jobs, this move was an ingenious blend of *chutzpah* and technology.[17]

The skirmish with Michael Eisner, however, did not die. Pixar did not renew its distribution contract with Disney under Eisner's watch. In the meantime, Eisner was forced to step down, officially retiring in 2005, and Robert Iger was named CEO. Jobs sent him a congratulatory e-mail, which led analysts and the media to speculate that with Eisner out of the way, Pixar would realign itself with Disney.

FUTURE VISION

Jobs revealed a very personal side of himself at a commencement address to Stanford graduates in June 2005. Using the metaphor of "connecting the dots" among critical points in his life, Jobs reflected on three key aspects: not finishing college, being thrown out of Apple, and confronting cancer.

Formal classroom learning did not match Jobs' lifestyle, and he didn't want to drain his parents' savings. He dropped out of Reed College after 6 months and left entirely after 18 months. He did, however, audit a class in calligraphy, and, while its immediate lessons were not apparent, it did give him the idea to make the Macintosh's on-screen fonts more appealing and more artistic.

Regarding his departure from Apple, in retrospect he says it "was the best thing that could ever have happened to me." The very public ousting challenged Jobs to refocus his priorities and "start over," leading him on a path of serial entrepreneurship with NeXT, the computer company, and Pixar, the animation company.

Finally Jobs spoke of being diagnosed with cancer. Fortunately his illness was treatable, and the earlier prognosis that he had only months to live was proven wrong. The experience, however, has been enduring, and he shared this with students: "Your time is limited, so don't waste it living someone else's life. Don't let the noise of others' opinions drown out your own inner voice. And, most important, have the courage to follow your heart and intuition." Jobs concluded his warm and candid remarks with something he recalled from the last issue of the *Whole Earth Catalog* by Stephen Brands, a publication that Jobs as a young man found inspirational. The quote is "Stay young. Stay foolish," and it has served as something of a guide for his own life as well as for the lives of the next generation of thinkers and doers.[18]

As for the future of Apple—analysts and skeptics have been debating this for years—no one knows. At one time, analysts wondered if it could survive as a niche computer maker—being indispensable to legions of graphic and Web designers, photographers, desktop publishers, and multimedia professionals. Today, the question still lingers, but powered by iPod and iMusic, Apple is generating revenues that enable it to stockpile cash and still pour money into research and development. "The great thing is that Apple's DNA has not changed." What has changed, according to Jobs, is that "the other side of the river is coming to us."[19] Technology with content and content with technology have converged and enabled Apple to leap to the forefront in ways that it was never able to do in the past. Jobs speaks of the new age of computing as a fusion of "designed applicability." Where it will lead, no one knows, but with prophets like Jobs, it will be a remarkable and sometimes loud journey.

For any leader confronting challenges and overwhelming odds, lessons can be learned by studying Steve Jobs' ability to frame, articulate, and market a world view. Jobs sums up the bottom line by saying that "Apple's core strength is to bring very high technology to mere mortals in a way that surprises and delights them and that they can figure out how to use."[20,21]

Leadership Lessons

- *Proclaim the vision.* Tell people where you are going. Get them to share in the excitement of it. Steve Jobs invites key stakeholders into his world vision and challenges them to dream the future with him.

- *Learn from others.* Look at what others are doing. Steve Jobs, like many technology people, believes that knowledge is a process of sharing what you know.

- *Hire the experts.* Surround yourself with people who can do what you cannot do. Throughout his career, Jobs has hired talented people; one (John Sculley) cost him his job, but many others have helped him grow the business.

- *Make a stand.* Let people know what your beliefs are. Jobs has stood with his Apple platform in the face of everyone telling him to abandon it. He's still here, and so is his company.

- *Live your message.* Steve Jobs is the embodiment of the new age entrepreneur, ready, willing, and able to commit himself and his resources to the pursuit of new ideas that will merge design and technology in ways that make it more accessible and usable and enjoyable.

"Good leadership can move mountains over a period
of time. Bad leadership can do great damage
overnight."[1]

Anne Mulcahy
CEO, Xerox

ALIGNMENT

TWO FOR ALIGNMENT

*It was never the hottest automotive company. That distinction
belongs to DaimlerChrysler, BMW, or even Porsche. It was
rarely a first mover, like Honda or Volvo. It is not the largest,
like General Motors. It suffers periodic earnings fluctuations,
like all heavy goods manufacturers. But it seems to be first
where it matters to customers seeking reliable everyday transportation. It is Toyota Motor Company.*

*In good times and in bad, Toyota stands astride the auto-
motive industry like an unstoppable juggernaut. You may liken
it to the Borg.* Star Trek *fans know the Borg as a culture of
humanoid drones operating under a single collective neural
processing unit that dictates thought, direction, and all actions.
Like the Borg, Toyota presents itself as a supremely aligned
organization. Unlike the Borg, which are destructive, Toyota is
constructive; Toyota makes some of the very finest cars and
trucks in the world. The company's goal is not world domination; it is increased market share. Its goal is 15 percent of the
world's market where only a few years ago it was 10. One more
thing, the Borg brook no dissent; Toyota thrives on it.*

*The myth of Japanese companies is their conformity—face-
less, bureaucratic, almost slavish. Conformity to a degree, yes,
but only after a decision has been reached. Whether the decision
is about what market to pursue or what component to improve,
there is much discussion, debate, and even disagreement. Once
the decision is arrived upon, parties put aside differences and
push forward, united in purpose. By contrast, all too often American companies squabble before, during, and after the decision
is made. Such dissension sabotages alignment.*

*"Toyota is a car company that challenges itself in a way
that makes the world shudder," asserts Maryann Keller, noted
industry analyst. "Toyota announces it is shooting for 15 percent of the global market and 50 percent cost cuts, and everyone goes 'Ooof!' It's like getting hit in the solar plexus."[2] That
gasp you hear is coming from competitors. Few senior auto
executives from competitors doubt that Toyota will be able to
achieve what it wants to achieve.[3] Pioneers of the Toyota Production System, which originated lean manufacturing (doing
more with less) and has expanded to flexible manufacturing
(building different models on same assembly line), Toyota is
moving to a new level of manufacturing that will enable it to cut
even more waste, time, and of course, costs.*

*Toyota, however, does not seek to cut costs like a samurai
swordsman, more like a sushi chef, delicately slicing here and*

there. Most important, the company works with its suppliers, and always has, to achieve mutually beneficial aims. The original equipment manufacturer (OEM)–supplier relationship, founded on keiretsu *principles, where companies have an equity stake in one another, is a further example of alignment.[4] When this system did not prove cost effective for emerging markets, Toyota gambled that it could export the principles of the Toyota Production System to suppliers in developing markets. Toyota is now engaged in a wholly new strategy for emerging markets with a new vehicle platform called IMV, for "innovative international multipurpose vehicle." Components for the vehicle, which can be configured as a truck, a sport-utility vehicle, or a minivan, will be made locally and cheaply in Asia and South America for those markets. Success in this venture will push Toyota toward its goal of 15 percent market share.[5]*

Toyota's global growth has not been without problems. Quality has become an issue. As the company grows, it is running short of its internally grown experts in the Toyota Production System. These highly trained experts implement the methods that distinguish Toyota as the leader in quality and efficiency. To make up for the shortage Toyota is looking to hire quality experts from its supplier network. You can liken this situation to a teacher who is looking to benefit from his or her students. As Art Nimii, a senior Toyota executive explains, "From here on, we are committed to operating around the world by using the combined capabilities of the Toyota Group as a whole. We may be running out of resources as a company, but as a group we still have plenty of resources."[6]

Toyota is willing to look inside its own bureaucracy to correct its deficiencies. Former president, Hiroshi Okuda, admitted that Toyota was too bureaucratic and held far too many meetings to keep people up to date. Under Okuda's direction, Toyota began to upgrade its information technology (IT) systems to improve not only internal communications but also its own knowledge management systems.[7] As legendary basketball player Wilt Chamberlain once commented about his public persona, "Nobody roots for Goliath." The same applies to Toyota, but when it comes to alignment, the company exemplifies what it means to pull together under a single vision and mission.

✑⑤ ⑤✑

Sometimes alignment emerges when you step out of line. In 2000, Pat Russo was a highly regarded executive with Lucent, an AT&T legacy company. Lucent had shed itself of everything but its division making equipment for phone manufacturers. When Russo was not offered the top spot, she took herself off the career path and left Lucent. After a short hiatus, she realized that she really would like to be a CEO. Kodak offered her its presidency, and she took the job. Immediately, she immersed herself in the tough job of a turnaround, complete with cutbacks and layoffs. Then, after less than a year on the job, her old company came calling; Lucent wanted her back, this time as CEO, so she realigned herself with her former employer.[8]

Going back may have been the easy part; discovering what she had to do was much harder—cut to grow. This is a kind way of saying shed business units, research and development, expenses, and of course, people. For someone who had grown up as she did at AT&T, where a job there was a job for life, it must have been a wrenching experience. But Russo was no stranger to making tough choices. She had made them throughout her fast-rising career. Cutting was not the sole answer. As she said in late 2004, "One way to [create value] is to cut your way to improvement, but that's not a long-term sustainable model. You've got to have some top line growth."[9] Operating in what some would call the unpredictable or even volatile technology sector, Lucent is pursuing growth in wireless technologies as well as VOIP (Internet telephony). The future may be promising, but Russo is too much of a realist to look too far ahead. "We're not focused on the future. We're focused on growing. We're focused on doing what we say. . . . That's our job."[10]

As a female CEO of a major company, Russo gets plenty of recognition, as well as plenty of criticism. Growing up as the only girl in a large Italian-American family, she learned to "roll with the boys." That is, she possesses superb communication skills; observers say that her presentations are clear and crisp, as you might expect of a CEO. Yet, unlike some more affable types, she does not share much of herself with the public. Insiders attest to her personal side; she's friendly, and she does have a weakness—chocolate.[11]

Customers have gotten to know her well; after returning to Lucent, she spent much of her time repairing relations with major customers. As she told Fortune *magazine then, "Nobody is going to give anything to us. We have to earn [customers'] business each and every day, in everything we do."*[12] *In the high-pressure technology sector in which Lucent competes, no one—customers, competitors, or investors—yields any quarter. Therefore, it is useful to have a person in charge who possesses a mastery of the business, as well as a feel for what makes it tick. That person is Pat Russo.*

ﻌﺌ ﻌﺌ

Alignment is where vision meets reality. For Toyota, alignment is the secret ingredient that holds a worldwide enterprise together. For Pat Russo at Lucent, alignment is what binds bright people together in the pursuit of current and future telecommunications technologies. For both Toyota and Lucent, alignment ensures that a vision can be implemented.

Alignment is the pursuit of getting everyone lined up to do what is necessary to achieve the vision and mission of the organization. An archetype of alignment is football. The goal of the game (vision) is to win. The mission is to win with the talents and skills you possess. Some teams have great running games; others excel at passing. Some do neither particularly well but succeed by mixing run and pass. The coaches draw up the game plans and assign roles to players. On offense, every player from quarterback to pulling guard, running back to wide receiver, tight end to center knows his position and what he must do. On defense, each player, under the nominal direction of the middle linebacker, has an assigned role. Their mission is to stop the offense. The highest point of alignment comes just prior to the snap of the ball when each player on offense and defense is in the right position. Once the ball is snapped, the game shifts from alignment to execution, a topic we will cover in the next chapter.

ALIGNING THE "RIGHTS"

Execution—and eventual results—cannot occur without people with the right talents, right skills, and right jobs being in a position to do their jobs. It is not enough to know where you want to go; it is often more important to know *how* you are going to get there. The leader must help lay the highway to the future by articulating goals, strategies, and objectives.

Alignment begins with putting the right people in the right slots. From a communications perspective, the leader must set expectations so that people know what must be done and what they need to do to contribute to achieving the vision. Expectations from managers typically are communicated one on one through e-mail or face-to-face communications. Anne Mulcahy at Xerox is a master at engaging her people with her communications; she tells the truth in hard times and pats them all on the back in good times. Her authenticity underscores her approach to management and has enabled Xerox to come back from the brink.

Talents and skills, as differentiated by authors Marcus Buckingham and Curt Coffman in their seminal book, *First, Break All the Rules*, describe two different capabilities. Talent is the nature of what one is born with; skills are the abilities one acquires along the way.[13] For example, Tiger Woods possesses two core talents—neither strictly tied to golf. The first talent is his willingness to work hard. He is relentless—spending hours and hours to master and remaster shots that he has done thousands of times before. The second talent is the desire to win; he seeks out the white heat of competition. The tougher conditions are, the more he relishes it. Why? Because he wants to win. His skills, by contrast, are his shot-making ability with the golf club, distance off the tee, ability to get out of trouble, and superior putting. When it comes to alignment, it is up to leaders to align people according to talents and skills.

COMMUNICATION REINFORCEMENT

Communication from more senior leaders can use the same channels, but the specifics of what needs to be done are handled by supervisors on the ground. And it is in the articulation of what needs to be done that people begin to take ownership of the vision and get aligned behind it. Take a quality initiative. The vice president of manufacturing will discuss the implementation of a Six Sigma program. The implementation of Six Sigma involves the training of cadres of black and green belt implementers, each with a specific task. Their roles are determined by emerging needs and assigned tasks. The net result of Six Sigma will be improved quality. The alignment begins with designation of the program and the assignment of candidates to implement it, each of whom takes ownership of the job.

Alignment demands adherence to mission. As stated earlier, mission is what the organization does to achieve its vision. It describes the products and services provided and why. Example: "Our mission is to provide food for people who want to lead healthier lives." Often these statements are coupled with a statement about the culture and mind-set of the people who work for the organization. "Our commitment to our customers begins with the commitment of our people dedicated to creating a people-first culture." Inherent in the mission is the commitment. More and more organizations are adding a commitment to ethics to their mission statements. "Our business principles are integrity and honesty. Our values reflect our commitment to the highest ethical standards."

FINDING THE MISSION AMONG THE GOALS

A mission statement is in essence a story outline, a quick synopsis of what a company does and what it stands for. The more descriptive the storyline, the better a company's leader can communicate alignment. By referring to a mission statement, a leader seeking alignment is stating the core of what a company does as it seeks to achieve its vision. Also, a mission statement adds clarity in terms of the products and services a company offers. And just as important, it emphasizes a company's commitment to aligning its culture and values with its vision.

There is a scene in the true-life movie *A Perfect Storm* when the captain asks his crew whether they want to wait out the impending storm or make a run for it. The decision is complicated by the fact that the ice machine is broken and their huge haul of swordfish is in danger of spoiling if they do not make it back to port soon. The entire crew desperately needs the money the catch will bring. Putting urgency ahead of caution, therefore, they agree to brave the hurricane and make a run for Gloucester. It is a fateful decision that will cost them their lives. While we can sympathize surely with their plight, from a management perspective, the captain, with acquiescence of the crew, was guilty of putting goals ahead of mission. The goal was to brave the storm and cash in on the haul; the mission was to earn a living as fishermen, even when it meant losing a catch but living to tell about it.

MISSION FIRST

Managers face such choices between mission and goal, thankfully not so dire, on a regular basis. Much of a manager's job is to impose order on the system. Order is expressed in the form of mission and objectives, as well as rules and regulations. While such discipline is absolutely necessary to efficient operations, many organizations become so wound up in procedure that they lose focus. Instead of stepping back and reflecting on the mission, they simply impose more regulation. By mission, I mean what an organization does and how it does it. For example, consider a quality-improvement initiative for a small-engine manufacturer. If you measure quality as fewer defects, you put your energy against that objective. If you think only in terms of reducing defects, however, you may be bringing down the total quality of the product. You run the risk of watering down performance for the sake of design simplicity only to end up with a lower-defect product with little appeal. Extreme case, perhaps!

When you emphasize one goal over another, you may sacrifice total performance for gain in a single attribute. This is precisely what happens in the world of dog breeding, a prime example of the law of unintended consequences at work. Breeding dogs for individual characteristics such as stance or shape of the ear will bring desired results, but along the way, you may pick up recessive genes that contribute to aggressiveness or genetic predisposition to injury and disease. People are not dogs, although some managers behave as if employees will respond to the sharp command or a swift kick as a canine might.[14]

HARMONIOUS ALIGNMENT

Goals and objectives in alignment with the mission are the metrics by which management measures performance. Sometimes, however, misalignment occurs between what is necessary for the job and what is necessary for the individual. While the ultimate measure of success is intended results, measurement must include the human factor. Ideally, you want results that satisfy the customer as well as satisfy employees. Such equilibrium is not always attainable, but it is a laudable outcome because over time satisfied employees will be able to contribute not only labor but also their ideas, which will lead to product improvement and continuing customer satisfaction. Developing goals in line with the mission is the role of every manager; communication can help in their development and deployment. Here are some suggestions:

- *Articulate the mission.* People need to know what business they are in. Take the U.S. Coast Guard; its mission is to protect our coastal waters from intruders, as well as protect people who use those waters. Among the heroes of the *Perfect Storm* saga were the New England–based Coast Guard pilots and sailors who ventured out into treacherous seas in response to calls for rescue. Coast Guard personnel put their lives on the line to save others; this is their mission, and they live it. Their officers, both commissioned and noncommissioned, articulate their mission so that it becomes ingrained within all ranks. Managers seeking to drill their mission home can learn from the way the Coast Guard does it—with constant communication in oral and written form backed by day-to-day example.

- *State the goals.* Giving people goals is essential to getting the job done. Successful people live for goals; they become energized by the achievement process. Part of the goal-development process must include the mission, of course. While managers are responsible for articulating the mission and developing baseline goals, employees should be encouraged to develop their own workplace goals in harmony. Health care is one industry that excels in this process. Health care providers work within a cost-regulated environment; managers and workers together find ways to deliver medical service in ways that not only satisfy patient needs but also deliver quality care at a reasonable cost. Ideas flow between management and staff as a means of finding balance between mission and goals, for example, taking care of patients.

- *Strive for balance.* As much as success-driven people love goals, you need to pull back the reins occasionally. After all, a laserlike focus on goals can burn holes in the mission. In other words, people become so focused on the task at hand that they lose perspective on the big picture, for example, developing a quality service, ensuring customer satisfaction, and making the workplace rewarding for employees. Unless a manager pulls an employee aside and says, "Hey, wake up and smell the coffee," the employee will keep drilling away on her assignment until she reaches China or dies of exhaustion, whichever comes first. Advice from a manager can help the employee gain perspective on the business as well as on herself. In order for goals to complement the mission truly, managers should try to find balance between professional and personal demands. When that balance is struck, the employee feels better about herself, as well as her work, and therefore is in a better position to become engaged, creative, and contributory.

FURTHERING THE MISSION

Goals must further the vision and mission; otherwise, you create misalignment within the organization, and things begin to go awry. There are moments, however, when goals must be achieved. Such situations occur in times of duress. For example, if a company is losing market share, it may need to revamp its product line to regain its competitive edge. It also may need to apply all necessary resources against this goal and may need to cut back in other areas such as marketing, training, and professional development. The mission remains to deliver a quality product with quality people, but sometimes that mission can be achieved only through such painful processes. Once the company stabilizes itself and brings another new product to market, it can reinvest in its people.

Investment in people, as a means of delivering on the mission, never really stops. Managers who communicate clearly and are attentive to their people nurture that investment. Their example articulates their faith not only in the capabilities of their people to do the job but also in their capacity to achieve the right outcomes. When mission and goals are in perspective, there is a harmony in purpose that ends up adding value where it matters in process and product and ultimately for the customer.

THE ROLE OF CULTURE

Culture is essential to driving alignment. The stronger the culture, the more apt people will be to get behind an initiative. Culture is the sum of norms, behaviors, guidelines, and values held by an organization. As mission defines what we do, culture defines who we are. While you often can summarize a culture as being people-focused, it goes beyond that. It is the soul of the organization: how it conducts business, how it treats its people, and how it delivers on the brand promise to its customers. For example, if a culture is one that insists on participation of employees in decision-making, gaining alignment may be slow going initially because people want to think about it and discuss it. If the culture is driven from the top down, apparent alignment will occur quite rapidly. Ultimately, however, lasting alignment will come from the participatory organization, because people generally support what they have a stake in. Compliance comes from being told what to do. Commitment comes from a shared vision.

The glue of culture is communications. Stories abound in such environments. 3M, for example, has a legacy of innovation. Its culture is one of active participation throughout the ranks. As a result, stories of innovation abound, the most famous being the story of the man who invented Post-It notes. Similarly, companies with a strong family ownership, such as Walgreen's, have a strong culture that is enriched by stories of its founder, Charles Walgreen, right up through today under the leadership of his successors, many of whom have been family members.[15] Stories nourish the culture and, by extension, the mission of the organization. The stronger the sense of mission, the greater are the opportunities to advance alignment!

ALIGNMENT IS STRATEGIC

Alignment is the linchpin between vision, mission, and execution. As such, it is the strategic enabler. Most organizations spend a great deal of time focusing strategic planning and the development and description of objectives and tactics that will enable people to achieve the vision. Alignment flows from the strategic plan because it marries the vision to the plan and subsequently to the execution. For example, Moses had the vision to lead his people to the Promised Land. His strategy was to vex the Pharaoh with a series of calamities ranging from beetles and drought to infanticide in order to motivate the Pharaoh to let his people go. All the Israelites were aligned behind Moses. The plan worked, and the Israelites escaped across the Red Sea. Once out of Egypt, Moses' followers wandered into the wilderness and even lost faith in Moses' leadership and their faith in God—so much so that Moses felt that they needed a form of realignment. It came in the form of the Ten Commandments. Adherence to the commandments steered the Chosen People back to righteousness and eventual arrival in the Promised Land. Moses himself never lived to see it, but by pointing his people in the right direction and keeping them aligned, he led them to the doorstep.

Communications is a key driver of alignment. It plays an essential role, ensuring that people follow the vision and stick to the mission. To drive alignment consider these steps:

- *Emphasize the mission.* Mission augments purpose. Adherence to mission is what alignment is really all about. Consider the example of Mary Sue Coleman, president of the University of Michigan, discussing the university's defense of its position on affirmative

action before the Supreme Court. While she was not
president when the suit was filed, she promptly backed
the university's stance, linking it to the university's
mission to provide for and deliver a diverse learning
environment for the benefit of current students and
society in general. Her statements reinforced alignment
within the university community and helped attract the
support of other organizations, such as the U.S. military, which submitted friend-of-the-court briefs on
Michigan's behalf.

- *Describe strategies.* A plan is just a plan if it remains
  uncommunicated. Referring to the narrative, leaders can
  prepare people for what's next. The leader sketches the
  big story and the spines, or strategies, that hold things
  together. A good way to communicate strategy is to distribute a form of the strategic plan to everyone. Let everyone have a look at it. Many organizations hold roll-out
  meetings around the strategic plan, enabling everyone to
  see what is expected of the organization and then contribute their ideas for how to make it happen. Stories arise
  from these gatherings. Collect them. They will help to
  guide the alignment process.

- *Link steps to actions.* The secret of alignment is action.
  Vision and mission together illustrate purpose. Alignment gives the process a backbone. It is up to the leader
  to communicate what needs to be done on a macro level
  and the managers to communicate on the team and
  department levels. Action steps emerge from the strategic
  plan. Grassroots planning from the supervisory ranks
  ensures that actions occur, but it is up to the leader to
  remind people continually that alignment implies action.
  Failure to link plan to action can spell disaster, as
  occurred with the federal government's tepid response to
  Hurricane Katrina.

- *Prioritize your action steps.* A key ingredient to alignment is prioritization, for example, knowing what you do first, second, and third and why you do it in that order. When Gary Nardelli became CEO of Home Depot, succeeding the charismatic founders Bernie Marcus and Arthur Blank, he realized that he would have to make some changes if the company was to fulfill its growth and earnings targets. It was the reason he was hired. Nardelli was forced to make some very unpopular moves that involved removing managers who did not hold to the new corporate vision. Nardelli and his team prioritized their tasks and put the big-box retailer on an aligned path to fulfill its growth targets.

- *Establish milestones.* A vision may represent a kind of Promised Land. But good visions take years to implement. Along the way, people need reinforcement and a reason to fulfill their mission. A way to reinforce this is by establishing milestones. The milestones mark progress: in products, from strategic intent and design through prototype, production, and distribution; in service, from strategic intent and design through alpha and beta testing and eventual implementation. Milestones, as will be discussed in Chapter 8, also serve as moments of celebration. Recognition of success is essential. Stories about what people did to achieve a milestone are essential to the development of alignment. It bonds people to the enterprise.

- *Keep the plan flexible.* Visions are not written in stone; they are written on stars. And guess what? Stars move. Visions, along with missions, often shift not so much in intent but in terms of feasibility. Markets shift, environments evolve, and good organizations respond accordingly. These alterations show up in alignment, making it harder to keep people focused. This is where the leader needs to be front and center, as well as in the middle, reminding people of the vision and mission and keeping people together. Flexibility is essential and healthy and, rather than an admission of something gone awry, is an example of firm and steady leadership.

These communication activities, reinforced through stories, make alignment tangible and enlist necessary support.

GUT CHECK

Just as alignment flows from vision, vision also can serve as the gut check of alignment. For example, if people are rallying to the cause, the vision has a good chance of moving forward. By contrast, if people are not getting behind it, then perhaps the vision needs to be reexamined. There always will be resistance to alignment because vision represents change, and alignment is the second step in the change process. Therefore, communications, buttressed by continual stories, serve to drive the process forward.

Alignment Story Planner

Alignment begins the process of getting people to follow the vision. Consider the following questions as thought starters to help the alignment process. Think of stories to support the alignment process.

- How will you emphasize the mission of the organization?
- How will you describe the strategies you want people to follow?
- How will you link alignment to results?
- What milestones will flow from the alignment process?

Communication Action Steps (Alignment)

- *Aspire.* Reiterate the vision.
- *Perspire.* Communicate the strategic plan.
- *Require.* Assign roles.
- *Transpire.* Articulate the necessity of pulling together.

ANNE MULCAHY

It is the nature of our society to fall in love with the new and different and to heap praise and lavish rewards on entrepreneurs who create and develop businesses. Part of the reason for this recognition is that entrepreneurs build on dreams and in the process create opportunities not only for themselves but also for an entire community. By contrast, relatively less attention is paid to executives who turn around failing businesses. There are exceptions, of course, but for the most part, outside the community where the business resides, such CEOs are relatively anonymous. There seems to be an expectation that it's their job, so they shouldn't expect any extra credit. Often the job of reviving a sinking business is more than a bailing act; it's an act of faith in people that involves a commitment to new ideas as well as courage to acknowledge mistakes of the past yet still move forward. Such is the case with Anne Mulcahy and Xerox.

An American icon of ingenuity, Xerox had invented the copier; its engineers had even helped to create the PC at Xerox PARC in Palo Alto. From the first business, it created an industry; from the second invention, it stood on the sidelines.[16] Thus, when low-cost copiers from Asia began to hit the U.S. market in the 1980s, Xerox's fortunes declined. In fact, a former chairman of Xerox once said that he knew that his company's business was in trouble when Japanese imports sold for less than Xerox could make them. Xerox did recover from that debacle with a commitment to quality and teamwork. In the process, it broadened its product line and got into data management. In short, Xerox was a resilient company, just like Mulcahy.

STRENGTH FROM FAMILY

Growing up in a household with four brothers, Mulcahy was treated as an equal. All the siblings shared in the household chores. As she told the *New York Times,* her father treated her mother as an equal; she ran the household finances. Her father did something else for the children; he instilled in them the value of ideas. Dinner table debates were common; topics ranged from "politics, religion, current events, anything that was contentious." While tempers would flare at times, those debates helped Mulcahy to define herself as a person who would live by—"and succeed because of—values, character, and intellect."[17]

Unlike most CEOs, Mulcahy never dreamed of becoming a CEO; she yearned instead to leave the company. Every time she bought a new briefcase, she promised herself that it would be the last one she would need.[18] Her husband, Joe, was a Xerox lifer and traveled extensively. They made an agreement that one or the other would stay home with their two boys while the other traveled. Mulcahy is grateful to the company for allowing her to carve out a sustainable work-life balance. In time, however, Mulcahy moved up the ladder, and her husband assumed more of the household responsibilities.[19]

TOUGH JOB

Mulcahy may not keep promises to herself, but she keeps them to everyone else, and this is why she was a perfect candidate to resurrect Xerox. In 2000, it was clear that the only place Xerox was going was down and down fast. It had over $17 billion in debt, $155 million in cash, and a stock price that was crashing (from a high of more than $60 to a low of less than $5). One of Xerox's senior leaders confided later that she was afraid that she would lose everything if Xerox tumbled. On the one hand, Mulcahy might have been too naive to say no to the CEO slot; a more hard bitten CEO type might have said thanks, but no thanks. "Most of us were looking ahead and not sensing what was about to happen," Mulcahy said of the crisis a few years later.[20] Still, this product of Catholic school education was no shrinking wallflower; what she was was dutiful, determined, and gutsy. She also was loyal. Her brother Tom Dolan is a 30-year veteran of Xerox, and her husband is a retired veteran of 35 years. She felt that she owed it to them and to all the people of Xerox to give her best.[21]

Bankruptcy was a real possibility; so was Chapter 11. Mulcahy would have none of it. Part of her reluctance may have stemmed from her in-depth knowledge of finance. She undertook a cram course in corporate finance under the tutelage of a senior Xerox finance manager. However, it was not the numbers that scared Mulcahy; it was the perception of what Chapter 11 would mean. She was more worried about morale than fiscal tightroping. Thus, as part of her effort, she met with 100 senior managers and asked for their commitment. If she was going to give it her all, they needed to do the same. Movement was essential; inertia was killing the company. As she said later, "We were 90,000 people sitting on the fence." One such senior manager was Ursula Burns, who had already taken a senior position with another company. She turned it down to stick with Mulcahy. It was Burns who spearheaded the operational review and streamlining that helped the turnaround effort.[22]

BELIEF IN PEOPLE

Mulcahy put her faith in people into practice with her communications. For Mulcahy, communication is a participatory process.

"It's telling people how they fit into the picture and listening to what's on their minds." Communication is also an act of courage. "It's taking the tough questions in front of a group of people and, when necessary, saying, 'I don't know.'" Her turnaround plan for Xerox emerged from communications with the rank-and-file. Once the plan was formulated, Mulcahy and her team focused on getting the message out in all employee meetings. To her credit, Mulcahy did not sugarcoat the issues facing Xerox; the future of the company was at stake. And, as she later recalled, her faith in people. "Through it all, we kept saying, 'We'll get through this.'" She also was straight with her people, never underestimating "how much [employees] were being asked to endure."[23]

And there was much to endure. The Securities and Exchange Commission (SEC) was investigating Xerox. For a company that prided itself on integrity, such scrutiny was a tough burden to bear, especially for Mulcahy, who once saw her picture in *Time* magazine alongside those of such questionable business tycoons as Dennis Kozlowski of Tyco and Bernie Ebbers of WorldCom. Eventually, Xerox settled with the SEC after agreeing to pay a $10 million fine related to accounting improprieties committed before Mulcahy became CEO. Still, the turnaround, as with all turnarounds, was not smooth sailing. For a while, bad news seemed to compound itself like bad earnings statements. Even Mulcahy, the true believer, had her doubts. She recalls coming back from a business trip to Japan and listening to a message from an old Xerox hand and chief strategist who complimented her on her efforts. Such a message gave her the impetus to continue.[24]

COMMUNICATIONS FIRST

Mulcahy is a passionate communicator—not in the sense of oratory but in the sense of commitment. Her presentations to employees during the turnaround are described by Ursula Burns as a "laying on of hands." Betsy Morris, who profiled Mulcahy for *Fortune,* labeled her commitment as one of "missionary zeal." Mulcahy also took a key step that most executives do not do; she personalized the communications. During business presentations, she appealed to employees' common sense: "Save each dollar as if it were your own." Mulcahy does not pull her punches, even when it could cost her. Shortly after becoming president of Xerox in 2000, she told financial analysts that Xerox had an "unsustainable business model." Xerox shares dropped 26 percent in one day. "Part of her DNA is to tell you the good, the bad, and the ugly." At the same time, she invests herself in the workplace; when employees see the top boss pulling her weight (and more), what employee is going to slack off?[25]

Skeptics thought that someone like Mulcahy, a lifer, would not have the stomach for the bloodletting that would need to be done. Mulcahy defied the critics; she rose to the challenge of the day and made the tough choices, one of which was to cut business units as well as people. More than 22,000 people were let go. For Mulcahy, it was not easy, but she put the needs of the organization, including remaining employees, retirees, and shareholders, first. "I am the culture. If I can't figure out how to bring the culture with me, I'm the wrong person for the job," she replied irately to a corporate lender. Xerox, to Mulcahy, was not simply a company; it was a cause as well as a family.[26]

Diversity for Mulcahy is not a nice-to-have; it's a reality. In a speech on the topic, she spoke of the many people in senior leadership positions who come from many different nations.[27] One of her key advisers is an African-American woman, Ursula Burns, who served as a confidant for Mulcahy during the turnaround effort. Mulcahy also can make jokes about the topic. When asked if she played golf, she replied that she did not, but that if she were invited to join Augusta National, a club with men-only membership, she would consider playing.[28]

Communication with the banking community was critical. Since Xerox's market capitalization had tumbled by 90 percent, bankers, who were owed billions, were on edge. One executive tells a story of Mulcahy giving a speech to more than 50 banks to which Xerox owed $7 billion. She received a stony reception, and as she sat down, she wondered, "What does it take to get a smile out of these guys?" The banker beside her quipped, "Seven billion dollars." Bankers do not value the warm and cuddly; they want assets and plans. And Mulcahy gave it to them. Under her leadership, Xerox paid down its credit line and put itself on a sounder financial footing.[29]

Customers also got the communications commitment. Things had eroded so badly for Xerox that some companies did not even include it on their bid lists; they feared that Xerox would go under. Mulcahy confronted the situation head on; she took to the road and met individually with key customers. In the process, she won many customers back to Xerox. She also focused on development and retention of the sales team.[30] After all, you cannot service customers effectively if your people are walking out the door.

PERSONAL COMMITMENT

One reason why Mulcahy climbed the corporate ladder was because she started in sales. "Having easily measurable results was hugely helpful. . . . You either succeeded or you didn't." Now, as a CEO, she is determined to help women in management move up if they earn it. "It's all about the pipeline and giving women the right experiences to get into top jobs." According to Mulcahy, all too frequently "women get sidelined to jobs that don't give them the experience required to get ahead." Those in a position to promote are also chiefly men. "People do make decisions around their comfort level." Even in her own company Mulcahy is not satisfied with the number of women in management. "We don't want to declare victory. . . . we're better than most . . . but we're not good enough."[31]

Mulcahy is a listener as well as a responder. Ultimately, every business rides the efforts of its people. Recognition is part of the Xerox culture. And when people write to Mulcahy, she replies to as many as she can; she does it for two reasons. First, she wants to acknowledge the suggestions of her people, and second, she considers it a form of recognition. Employees will tell her, "I can't believe you wrote me back." She also did something more; employees who toughed it through with her get their birthdays off. It is all part of how Mulcahy provides energy and direction to the company.[32]

Mulcahy is a people person. She claims that she enjoys herself the most when she is meeting and mingling with Xerox employees. Formal presentations are not her thing; she wants to hear what's on peoples' minds. In this give and take she knows that people can feel her commitment as she feels theirs. Their personal "stories" provide energy not only to Mulcahy but to everyone in the company.[33] And in turn, these narratives, which tell of hard work, discipline, and success, have enabled a once-proud company to return to prominence.

Leadership Lessons

- *Play it straight*. Employees deserve the facts. Anne Mulcahy is a straight shooter; she does not soft pedal bad news but shares it with everyone.
- *Stay on message*. Communication is hard work. It takes time to articulate goals, strategies, and tactics.
- *Listen to your people*. Like all good leaders, Mulcahy knows that if you want people to follow you, you had better listen to them and their ideas.
- *Focus on customers*. When business at Xerox was eroding, Anne Mulcahy took to the road to revitalize flagging customer relationships. It was a strategy that worked.

(Continued on next page)

- *Commit to the work.* Turning around a sinking ship is not easy. Mulcahy invests herself in the business and works hard to succeed.

- *Believe in your people.* When Xerox was struggling, Mulcahy knew that if Xerox was to survive, it would have to do it with the people on its team.

- *Insist on discipline.* Good leaders like Mulcahy hold people accountable for their actions. Such accountability has enabled the company to turn disaster into opportunity.

- *Be passionate.* Anne Mulcahy regards Xerox as family; she is committed to the people of the company and its culture.

Perspire

- *Execution—what the organization needs to do*
- *Discipline—how the organization stays the course*

*I*t is one thing to plan; it is another thing to fulfill the plan. That demands enormous commitment. The leader therefore must demonstrate what it takes to do the job and participate in the process so that people stay focused on the task as well as the goal. Execution then becomes a balancing act between aspiration and perspiration.

C H A P T E R

"Execution is the tough, difficult, daily grind of making sure the machine moves forward. . . . Accountability must be demanded, and when it is not met, changes must be made quickly."[1]

Lou Gerstner
Who Says Elephants Can't Dance?

EXECUTION

TWO KINDS OF EXECUTION

In an instant, the buildup was over. Discussion was moot; the nation was at war. Within hours of the decapitation strike against Saddam Hussein's regime, coalition ground forces, chiefly American and British, streamed across the border into Iraq. Over the skies of Baghdad, U.S. fighter jets unleashed thousands and thousands of guided bombs to preselected targets. Commentators drooled that no general in history, from Alexander to Julius Caesar, Napoleon Bonaparte to Irwin Rommel, Stonewall Jackson to George Patton, had ever taken as much territory in so little time.

Through it all, American television carried the war live to living rooms back home. For the first time we saw battles in real time. And while U.S. networks did not carry footage of American soldiers dying, Aljazeera did, along with many more hours of Iraqi civilian casualties. The net effect was to galvanize American opinion solidly behind, if not the president, then certainly the American troops.

It was not a flawless march into Baghdad. Aside from the casualties, which compared with wars past were remarkably light, there was a degree of second-guessing among commentators, many of whom were retired military officers working on camera for the networks. An off-hand remark by the chief U.S. ground forces commander, William Wallace, admitting that troops had not "war-gamed" against some of the scenarios fueled speculation that we were fighting the war on the cheap and could not prevail without more and more troops and materials. Within days, or at most a week, these objections faded into oblivion as U.S. troops took the Baghdad airport and encircled the city. Despite the lunatic assertions of the Iraqi information minister, nicknamed "Baghdad Bob," U.S. forces took the city within days, and throughout the nation, statues of the dictator were being pulled down, some with the assistance of the U.S. military.

The ebb and flow of the battle seen mostly from afar but all too often up close via satellite videophones gave observers a lesson into execution. While politicians bickered and American public opinion swayed to and fro, the military did its job. American soldiers executed, not flawlessly, but with courage and conviction. They braved the surprisingly strong pockets of resistance, and they pushed onward. This was execution on both macro and micro levels, and it was made possible by boots on the ground and wings in the air, as well as thousands of support troops on ships and in bunkers hundreds of miles away. Everyone pulled together in a magnificent showing of bravery, tenacity, and sheer determination. Execution, you bet!

Unfortunately, the brilliant execution of the successful attack was dimmed by the postattack ground operations; Iraqis bent on enriching themselves as opposed to their nation looted public facilities, including office buildings, hospitals, universities, and public utilities. With insufficient troops on the ground, coalition forces could not stop the looting. Soon insurgent forces, fueled by radicals from abroad as well as home-grown terrorists, fought running battles with coalition forces, inflicting thousands of casualties. Our troops continued to execute their mission, however, striving to keep the peace as well as helping to rebuild the infrastructure. Within a year, the tide at home began to turn against the war, but respect for U.S. troops—undermanned and under-armored—only grew. Our soldiers continued to execute, despite successive waves of suicide bombings and skirmishes aimed at destroying them. Our troops are training and building an Iraqi defense force, and their presence enabled Iraqis to hold free elections in January 2005. Only time will tell if the world will remember our troops' execution as well as their years of sacrifice.

⁂

Sometimes execution comes down to the example of a single individual.

When it came to his chosen profession, there is no one better. His colleagues in the business admitted that he had taught them most of what they knew. He was friends with a president. His hobbies all had something to do with speed—stock car racing and later boat racing. He was played in a movie by none other than John Wayne. His favorite color was red, and he had it painted on all of his equipment. He also took it as his nickname, Red Adair, oil firefighter extraordinaire.

Red Adair got his start in the business almost by accident, as if there is any other way to get involved in fighting oil fires. It was in Smackover, Arkansas, that Red first encountered what would become his life's work. A well was burning out of control, and the firefighters had fled. Someone put a question to Red, "Boy, do you want to work and make some money?"[2] Red approached the wellhead and single-handedly stopped the flow of natural gas and extinguished the fire. From that moment on he was hooked on his chosen career. However, he did take time out to serve in World War II, at what might be one of the few jobs more hazardous than his own—bomb disposal. It was there that he learned two important lessons: proper use of explosives and keeping an even temper.[3]

To say that fighting oil fires is a dangerous business is an understatement—it is an extremely dangerous occupation. But if you know what you are doing, you can minimize the risks. "If you were in his presence, you were going to do it his way. He was very demanding," says Patrick Campbell, CEO, of Wild Well Control. Campbell credits Adair with educating the industry on proper ways to fight fires. While working with Myron Kinley, another legend in the industry, Adair pioneered the use of dynamite to put out oil fires; it was akin to fighting fire with fire. Properly placed and timed explosives would deny the fire what it needed—oxygen and fuel.[4]

While Adair created a name for himself in Texas, he furthered his reputation by fighting oil fires at sea and in the desert. He was the first to extinguish a fire on an off-shore oil platform, and in 1962, he put out the famed "Devil's Cigarette Lighter" fire that had been burning in Algeria for six months. John Glenn said that he saw that fire's flames from space during his orbits around the earth.[5]

Adair's greatest acclaim came in 1991 when he was called in to put out what no one else could do—the burning oil fields of Kuwait that Saddam Hussein's troops had ignited during their retreat. Some have described it as hell on earth; smoke rising to 15,000 feet, extreme heat at the wellhead topping 3000°F, and *negligible visibility. It also was costly—5 million barrels ($150 million) per day going up in flames. It was no match for Red, who called on friend, President George H. W. Bush, to get him the bulldozers and cement he needed and then went to work. In his own self-assured but self-deprecating way he said, "We put all the fires out with water, just went from one to the other." What Adair and his team did was pump sea water into the pipes. Fires that some feared would burn for three to five years were dampened by Red's crew in nine months.[6]*

Adair was always a good story. He courted the media, and they courted him back, a practice that has been discontinued since oil companies do not like to advertise the fact that their wells (and assets) are going up in smoke. Dave Ward, a television news anchor who covered Adair's adventures for years, summed up his good friend this way: "He always set out to do what he said he'd do. He never had a well he didn't get under control, and he never lost a single man."[7]

Another friend, Bum Phillips, former NFL football coach, had a favorite story about his friend. As the tale goes, a Texan was at the pearly gates of heaven and annoying Saint Peter something fierce, likely because he was bragging up his home state. So Saint Peter showed him a picture of the fires of hell and asked if there was anything like that in Texas. To which the man replied, "Nope. But we have a guy who can put it out, and that's Red Adair."[8]

❦

A famous movie director once said that directing a movie was as simple as falling off a log. His comment was not totally in jest. For him, the act of direction was a logical progression from good story, excellent script, strong preproduction, gifted actors, and skilled technicians. In other words, his direction both facilitated and benefited from superb execution.

Execution is not easy. In fact, execution is often what separates vision from reality. Visions that stay in the stars are visions that were poorly executed. To conceive a vision and align people behind it requires insight, imagination, and the ability to communicate. It also requires fortitude and perseverance, along with discipline (to be discussed in Chapter 5), to execute well. This is the lesson the U.S. Army delivered during the invasion of Iraq and that Red Adair delivered in his lifetime of fighting the world's most treacherous fires.

As hard as execution is, it is well worth it because execution delivers the goods—the results promised in the vision and buttressed through alignment. However, as with so many good things in life—running a company, managing a hospital, being a principal, or coaching a team—it is execution that demands the heavy lifting. Execution often eats people up in terms of concentration, effort, and time. Execution is plain exhausting.

Some of the best examples of execution emerge from sales. Salespeople have an innate drive to execute; they are responsible for putting the offer to the customer—presenting, negotiating, and closing the deal. Execution for them is essential. They live by metrics—quotas in terms of sales calls, sales visits, sales presentations, sales follow-ups, and sales made. Furthermore, the sales organization is numbers-driven in terms of figures for sales calls made, sales logged, and revenues generated. As a final step in the business process, salespeople work with what they are given in terms of product or service and marketing support. They also deal in the real world—not off marketing diagrams and flowcharts. They deal with customers who may like or dislike the offering, may be predisposed to another product or another vendor, or may be coping with a declining budget. Salespeople often are independent-minded, but in large organizations, they learn to pull together with other functions in marketing, logistics, and distribution to serve customer needs. The bottom line is that salespeople deliver results. They are superb at execution.

One reason for their success lies in their communication skills. Salespeople are good listeners; they also read people well. Salespeople know how to present an offering with benefits that appeal to what buyers like. Salespeople often are natural storytellers, and their stories revolve around the sales process. Sales managers often train people themselves. They conduct role-plays for varying customer conditions, coaching new hires how to act and what to say and backing them up with frequent feedback. Sales leaders become strong leadership models, ones who value the contributions of their team and use their communications to teach, coach, and inspire their people.

DELEGATION DRIVES EXECUTION

Execution begins with communication. "What am I supposed to do?" is a question that echoes in the halls and cafeterias of underperforming organizations. This complaint is not something you hear from slackers; you will hear it from the most dedicated people in the organization. It is the most basic question that deserves the most basic answer because it encapsulates exactly what an employee is supposed to do with his time. And when it is not answered succinctly, logically, and with forethought, it creates a situation more akin to an anarchist convention than a business organization, that is, a bunch of people sitting around with too much time on their hands.

Situations like this arise for a variety of reasons: reorganization, merger, and the appointment of new managers. There is a common thread found in each instance, and it stems from a failure to delegate. On one level, delegation is the assignment of tasks to employees; on another level, delegation is the granting of responsibility and authority. Both levels require something very basic to hold them together: communication that provides information as well as invites participation:

- *Brief people on what needs to be done.* Employees cannot do what they do not know. Recall the pilot briefings you have seen in war movies or more recently on television news. Note how the commander describes the mission and objectives and then makes assignments. Managers can do the same. When new projects are assigned, gather your people together. Overview the scope of the work and what is expected of the group. Make assignments then or in subsequent one-on-one meetings.

- *Invite participation.* Management is about getting things done. Leadership is about getting others to do what needs to be done. When you delegate assignments, give people a voice in the process. Sometimes you can ask the person if she is interested in doing the job; other times you will not have that luxury. When you make the assignment, do not tell people *how* to do the job. Let them work that out for themselves. Be available for advice, but do not advise unless asked or unless the project is going terribly awry. You may ask for a plan of action in advance and comment accordingly. Recall this model the next time you must present an implementation plan to senior management.

- *Confer responsibility.* The outcome of delegation is consequence. Managers must make certain that people know that they are responsible for the work and the results. Responsibility is one part burden and another part recognition. You must have both elements for people to want to assume the responsibility for mobilizing other people to action and equipping them with the tools they need to do the job. Responsibility breeds ownership, and in management, ownership of a project is paramount.

- *Grant authority.* The essence of delegation is the authority to do the job. When you make someone a project leader, make certain that others on the team know who's in charge and who has the authority to make decisions. Never assume that everyone knows; you must make it known to the team, either orally or in writing, preferably both. Giving authority to a trusted employee accomplishes three things: (1) it enables the team leader to make decisions, (2) it signals to the team that you are willing to share responsibility, and (3) it develops leaders for the future.

USING CONVERSATION FOR UNDERSTANDING

Experienced managers may be thinking so far so good, but what about employees who do not know what you want them to do? Again, it's a matter of communication. Engage the person in a conversation. Begin on a positive note with a comment about the quality of work the individual has been doing. Then move in to the specifics: Ask the person if he is doing what he agreed to do? Sometimes the employee may be trying to do the work, but someone (a coworker) or something (a process) is preventing him from doing the job. Find out why. If it's a management issue involving people and processes, fix it. If the employee wants to be doing something else, ask why? Perhaps the current assignment is not challenging enough or is too challenging. You will only discover the answer by asking.

Sometimes the very fact that you take the time to listen makes all the difference in the world. The work must be done, but see if you and the employee can come up with alternatives in scheduling, resources, or personnel. Of course, if you try all these steps and work is still not getting done, then you may have to invite the employee to consider working in another department or another organization. Management requires discipline tempered by the human condition, but it is still a discipline. You are accountable for the results, so you need to get things done right.

Delegation is essential to good management, but it is surprising how often it is overlooked or ignored. Taking the time to have a conversation with an employee about what she should be working on is critical to getting things done. Encapsulating the conversation in the form of action steps or performance objectives may be even more valuable. And taking the time to listen to each other, both boss and employee, may be the secret of effective delegation because both parties have the opportunity to share ideas and issues as a means of moving forward. Communication is integral to delegation; it drives the process as well as holds it together.

DRIVING EXECUTION

Communication, enriched by ample stories, can focus people on performing the task at hand, which is what execution is all about. Communication weaves its way through execution and pushes it along. Lou Gerstner is not the most gregarious of executives, but he was crystal clear in his communications; he articulated his strategies to his top lieutenants and expected them to be carried out. Tactics were up to the executives to figure out. And they did.

- *Take action steps.* Alignment involves assigning the right people to the right tasks. Execution involves pushing the go button and letting things fly. Take a well-honed marketing plan that articulates all the steps involved in promoting the product. The action steps put plans to action. The ad agency executes the commercials and print ads. The public affairs people execute the key messages. The marketers execute the merchandising. Execution is action.

- *Manage teams.* Alignment dictates the marshalling of masses to do the jobs. Often the jobs are team efforts. Over recent decades, self-managed teams have worked well in all kinds of endeavors from research through engineering and maintenance. The self-management grants the team a sense of autonomy, and often it enables teams to work very efficiently. Other endeavors, either by custom or by necessity, feature more hands-on management. Whatever the method, communication is essential between team members and the team leader. Also, managers can network among themselves to garner resources as well as best practices.

- *Follow up.* It is up to the leader to ensure that things get done—that execution really is generating results. This activity involves much communication. Asking questions and insisting on thorough briefings from employees is not a form of meddling. It is engagement in the process that ensures execution. Product-development team leaders learn quickly that when they leave things too much alone, they don't get done. Therefore, they get involved.

LEAD BY LETTING GO

So much of leadership is supporting others, pushing them to success. As discussed earlier, delegation of responsibility and authority plays an essential role. All too often managers are given the responsibility of getting things done but no resources or authority to get them done. This is a failure of delegation. It indicates one of two things: Either the manager is not aware that others require authority or, more often, the manager fears the loss of personal authority and keeps it tightly guarded. This situation is paralytic. The one delegated to do the work cannot do it properly, and the manager who hoards authority feels that he must manage every detail.

Supervision is a form of leadership by letting go. Just as parents must say good-bye to their children in varying degrees from preschool through university and eventually their own places to live, managers must say good-bye to micromanagement. As with parenting, the letting go represents freedom; children are free to learn and grow and develop their own lives. Managers who let go of the reins with their employees enable them to develop skills and move into more senior roles. And guess what? Again, as with parents, adults and managers rediscover themselves and new challenges. Micromanagement is very hard on the employees and in a way worse on the manager because it binds the manager to her limitations. By never letting go, she remains locked within her own capabilities; she never grows. She never enables her people to execute to their abilities, and results come in fits and starts, if they come at all.

Leading by letting go is simple to express but very hard to live by because it involves a form of dual trust. The manager must trust his people with the responsibility and authority, and he also must trust himself to learn to step back. So many times the manager who means well will jump back in at the first hint of trouble. Like the preschool mother who helps her child put on his coat, the unsure manager will leap in to button things up. Such assistance may be beneficial for children, but not always for employees.

From a communications perspective, managers need to share their experiences with one another on this topic. Management courses do not cover it adequately, and here is where the sharing of experiences, through storytelling, can make the letting-go process more acceptable and tangible. And most important, it builds greater levels of trust throughout the organization.

EXECUTION IS FULFILLMENT

Execution is a grind, yes. But the reward—be it a winning product, a superior hospital, a school of motivated kids, or a victory in a game—is sweet. Execution flows from vision and alignment and involves implementing plans on paper into plans that serve people either as products or as services. There is dignity in execution that is often taken for granted or overlooked entirely. This sense of higher purpose emerges from the sacrifice required to fulfill the vision and support the mission. It often means that a great many people have gotten behind the effort, often putting aside their individual pursuits in the attempt to deliver on something greater than themselves. There is true nobility in that kind of execution. And there are great stories to tell about it.

Execution Story Planner

Execution moves vision and alignment into results. Consider the following questions as a means of helping you to drive execution. Think of stories to support the execution process.

- What are the first action steps you will take? Why?
- How will you ensure that teams drive the execution process? How and why will it be important?
- How will you follow up to ensure that people are doing what they are supposed to be doing? What will you do if they are not doing it?
- How will you discipline yourself to lead by letting go?

Communication Action Steps (Execution)

- *Aspire*. Hold fast to the vision.
- *Perspire*. Link alignment to execution.
- *Require*. Reiterate what needs to be done.
- *Transpire*. Push, push, push.

LOU GERSTNER

It is not often that, when an executive retires, part of his "going-away package" includes an apologia (albeit lightheartedly) from a member of the business news media. Well, it is not every day that Lou Gerstner retires as CEO of IBM after masterminding one of the most successful transformations in history. And it is not every day that Stewart Alsop, a respected columnist for *Fortune* magazine, writes an open letter to Gerstner offering to "eat my words" for doubting that Gerstner was the right man for the job. Alsop, along with many on Wall Street and in the media, did not consider the former McKinsey consultant, former senior executive at American Express, and former CEO of RJR Nabisco as suitable material for the top slot in one of America's venerable institutions. After all, as Alsop notes, what did Gerstner know about technology? As it turned out—plenty.[9]

TROUBLE INSIDE IBM

Truth be told, Gerstner was one of a handful of top executives considered for the helm of IBM. Reports were that both Jack Welch of General Electric and Larry Bossidy, then of Allied Signal, had said no—and with good reason. IBM in 1993 was not the same high-growth, technical wizard that had equipped the world's largest companies with its computer hardware. By this time, the PC revolution had swept global computing and in the process had changed the way executives view information technology (IT). Information was power, and everyone wanted that power on his or her desk via their desktop. IBM was slow to accept the PC revolution, but it had other problems as well—lack of vision, strategy, and execution. As usual, it was people who bore the brunt of IBM's missteps. By 1994, IBM would have laid off nearly half its workforce. This was heresy to a company that prided itself on cradle-to-grave employment. Internally, IBM was roiling, but on the surface, all seemed normal to the old hands. Sam Palmisano, Gerstner's eventual successor but at the time of this statement head of what would become global services, said: "Meetings would go fine. . . . [A] bunch of people would sit around have a nice chat." Good results or bad, the evaluation was the same, "Thank you very much." Of course, if the results were bad, they would add a caveat: "We know you tried your best."[10]

Word was out, and Gerstner wanted no part of IBM, but IBM wanted him badly. "Lou was tougher than nails. Hard things needed to be done, and I knew he could do them," said IBM director James E. Burke, former CEO of Johnson & Johnson. "We needed someone who was by instinct, training, and interest very strategic in his thinking." While Gerstner resisted, he was vulnerable on one count—a sense of patriotism. Those recruiting him positioned the job as one, wrote Betsy Morris for *Fortune,* that was a "moral imperative"—"for the good of the country." Burke was even more blunt to Gerstner: "You owe it to America to take the job." The nation could not stand losing the blue chip company that had sold mainframe computing to the world. Ironically, many insiders, as well as those on Wall Street, thought that while IBM should remain, it should be pared down piece by piece. The insiders got their man but not their sell off strategy.[11]

TOUGH GUY

Lou Gerstner was not an executive who paid much attention to other people's strategies. He rose to the top of his game by being tough and pugnacious, as well as savvy and very shrewd. Born on Long Island into a working-class household, his parents instilled in him a sense of excellence. That drive was honed by discipline at Chaminade, a noted Catholic college preparatory school. Fellow student Robert Wright, later head of NBC and vice chairman of General Electric, said of the discipline, "Do it once, stay late. Do it twice, leave school." Those who pushed it further were expelled. Gerstner excelled and won a scholarship to Dartmouth. He then matriculated to Harvard Business School, and later he worked for McKinsey & Company, a top-flight management consulting firm, where he became a partner at the young age of 28. Gerstner had brains as well as the determination to back them up. And he would need every ounce of that determination to make it at IBM.[12]

For one thing, he was an outsider; he began his tenure with only an executive assistant. Thus he relied on the advice of others; this can have its hazards for a newbie, even one as astute as Lou. "There's no question that, during the first year, there were some attempts to feed me intellectual arsenic—some bad ideas, some pet projects." One hedge was to bring in some senior-level talent in finance, marketing, legal, and public relations. Gerstner, a veteran of turnarounds at American Express and RJR Nabisco, commented later, "It's extremely helpful having some people you can shorthand and rely on because you know them well." Still if IBM, like any large organization, were to succeed, it would have to rely on the people inside the company, the veterans who had been with the company during the glory days as well as the dog days. Gerstner sought out that talent and promoted it. One former executive from RJR Nabisco summed up his former boss's working style this way: "He gets everyone to buy into the strategy, and then doesn't micromanage. If you expect to be stroked, forget it." What Gerstner does, however, is mentor. "I work hard at helping people improve their skills, grow, and get better at what they do." In other words, Gerstner's style is to challenge rather than give "atta boys." Recognition, however, does come in the form of compensation; he set records at IBM with bonuses.[13]

COMEBACK STORY

The revival of IBM has a private face and a public one. After agreeing to come aboard, Gerstner met with senior leadership. He played it straight, relating a series of expectations as well as some key action steps for the first 90 days. These are itemized in his personal account of his sojourn at IBM, *Who Says Elephants Can't Dance?* Reading over the account, you get a crystal-clear expectation of what he wanted to accomplish. For example, IBM would need to get a handle on cash flow, attend to customer needs, and develop the right strategy. As part of this meeting, Gerstner addressed the human equation. He gave the senior managers a peek into his leadership style, which includes such things as "manage by principle," belief in "strong competitive strategies and plans, teamwork," and "pay for performance." He also shared one of his mantras: "Move fast." In this talk, he also asked his senior leadership team to buck up. "It is not helpful to feel sorry for ourselves. I'm sure our employees don't need any rah-rah speeches. We need leadership and a sense of direction . . . not just from me but from all of us."[14]

The public side of the revival did not go so smoothly. At his first public press conference after three months as CEO, he uttered the quote that may become his epitaph: "There's been a lot of speculation as to when I'm going to deliver a vision of IBM, and what I'd like to say to all of that is that the last thing IBM needs right now is a vision." He then went on to itemize four key priorities related to profitability, customer focus, strategic direction, and solutions orientation. It was the vision statement that garnered the most publicity and none too positive; he was criticized as too focused on cutting, too strategic, too inward-focused, and even, according to *The Economist,* "short-sighted." Gerstner bristled at the criticism, but in hindsight, he was totally correct. In his book he also clarifies the comment to include the words "right now," which were dropped from many transcripts. The reason that these two words are important, according to Gerstner, is that IBM had many vision statements developed by insightful people; the problem was not foresight, it was about not getting things done. "Fixing IBM," he writes, "was all about execution." Furthermore, Gerstner states that it was time to stop finding "people to blame"; rather, it was a time for a "sense of urgency."[15]

One of the first things that Gerstner did was dismantle the management committee. At one time, this committee served as a vetting ground for new ideas and technologies in which the company should invest. It was a good idea, but like many good ideas that are not reinvigorated over time, the management committee had ossified. Rather than a gateway, it served as a roadblock to new ideas. This committee served as a kind of power behind the throne. By abolishing it, Gerstner would have more direct control over corporate direction. For Gerstner, however, it was not strictly about power; it was about *change.* IBM would have to become more customer-focused. This is easy to say but very difficult to do, especially in a large organization like IBM, where power was entrenched in silos divided by business units as well as geography.[16]

What Gerstner and his team did was to push IBM to adopt the customer viewpoint. Again, most companies say this, but few can do it. What it meant for IBM was shifting from becoming a purveyor of hardware to a purveyor of services that integrated software solutions and hardware. Long known for hooking a customer into an IBM system to the exclusion of all others, IBM moved from that model into doing what the customer wanted, including integrating hardware from other vendors into a customer network. This was heresy to the old IBM but gospel to the new IBM. Why change? Because the market had changed. IT had evolved from stand-alone special-access mainframes to networks of distributed intelligence that integrated hardware, middleware, and applications software. Put another way, IT professionals in organizations became solutions providers to their internal customers who needed to process their own data for their own function, be it finance, marketing, or engineering. And, of course, everyone needed e-mail access. Incidentally, IBM was a pioneer with its proprietary PROFS system, which many corporations used in the pre-Internet days.[17]

By 1995, revenues at IBM began to increase, and by 1997, Gerstner was being regaled as a hero for righting the ship. Gerstner was not done. As he wrote, "Our greatest ally in shaking loose the past . . . was IBM's own precipitous collapse." Gerstner felt that to keep IBM moving forward, he needed to keep a "sense of urgency" paramount. After all, the Internet boom was just about to hit, and IBM would not miss this trend as it had missed other IT evolutions in the recent past. eBusiness became another avenue for IBM to demonstrate its customer focus and continue to provide hardware, software, and network solutions for customers in both virtual and nonvirtual environments. In other words, IBM would exert its leadership as it had in the past and would do so again.[18]

MAKING LEADERSHIP PERSONAL

Fundamental to Gerstner is personal leadership—being visible and available. Gerstner writes that "the best leaders create high-performance cultures." It does not occur by happenstance; rather, it happens when "great CEOs roll up their sleeves and tackle problems personally." Such leaders do not "hide behind staff." "They are visible everyday with customers, suppliers, and business partners." What propels such leadership is "communication, openness, and a willingness to speak often and honestly, and with a respect for the intelligence of [others]." Respect for employees means giving them "bad news" personally, as well as giving them the right "to understand what's going on in the enterprise." Passion drives Gerstner's leadership persona; he believes that it is the most vital aspect of personal leadership. For Gerstner, passion translates into "making things happen and winning, winning, winning." Leaders must project that passion, but at the same time they must augment it with leadership fundamentals such as "accountability," "participation," and "visibility," as well as business fundamentals such as strategy and execution. In other words, there was discipline and rigor in the passion that gave it teeth and made it something that could be "measured" and delivered on.[19]

For all his virtues, however, there is no question that Gerstner has rough edges that everyone from fellow CEOs to former colleagues acknowledge grate on them. Words such as *arrogant* and *pompous* are descriptors that others use. Gerstner makes no apologies. "If you wanna know if I'm intense, competitive, focused, blunt, and tough, yes. That's fair. I'm guilty."[20] He is not one for small talk, but he is one who makes things happen.

Gerstner proves in his book, *Who Says Elephants Can't Dance?* that he has a flair for storytelling. By blending story points with occasional dot points that reflect either his strategies or his action steps, Gerstner sketches a comeback story like no other. As storyteller-in-chief, Gerstner spins a tale in which the people of IBM saved the company and in the process saved their livelihoods, as well as the products and services the company provides to customers around the world. Without Lou Gerstner, IBM might be a shell of what it is today or not even around. In his apologia, Stewart Alsop states, "IBM didn't need a vision; it needed to execute smartly for its legions of customers." This is exactly what Gerstner had been saying for his near-decade at the helm. And so, when a journalist says it in praise, you know you've done something right. And that's quite a story.[21]

Leadership Lessons

- *Be open to ideas*. Lou Gerstner took the helm of IBM with a good sense of strategy and execution, but he knew that revitalization could only come by working with people, not against them.
- *Communicate relentlessly*. The success of IBM depended on the commitment of everyone in the company. One of the best ways to push for commitment is to communicate the why and how of what people need to do frequently.
- *Live for execution*. Execution is the art of getting things done. Lou Gerstner drove execution by setting expectations, holding people accountable, and rewarding them accordingly.
- *Drive to win*. Every leader must, as Gerstner says, "make things happen." The outcome should be a will to win the right way, with strategy, execution, and good people.
- *Make passion real*. Lou Gerstner believes that passion is essential to leadership. He links that passion to principles of management and leadership to ensure that it has meaning and can be acted on.

C H A P T E R

"I have to make decisions in the best interest of the football team. I can't answer to one particular constituency. . . . I have to make a decision. Whether the players understand that or respect that, I don't know. I hope they do. I think they do."[1]

Bill Belichick
Head Coach, New England Patriots

DISCIPLINE

*L*OOKING BACK WITH THE HINDSIGHT OF MORE THAN A CENTURY, *it seems that human beings have always flown. Until December 1903, however, what we take for granted today was considered possible only by a handful of people and by most as fanciful. It took the persistence, diligence, and dogged determination of two bicycle mechanics from Dayton, Ohio, to* *turn disbelievers into believers. And it did happen overnight; it was a conquest of the air that required self-study, relentless experimentation, and above all, discipline.*

Through the lens of folkloric history, the Wright Brothers might appear to be a couple of lucky bumpkins who discovered how to fly. Nothing could be further from the truth. As James Tobin paints their story in his remarkable history, To Conquer the Air, *Wilbur Wright was a driven man possessed by the desire to fly but steeled inside by willingness to study flight in all its aspects and commit himself, and later his brother, Orville, to his vision of powered flight.*

If humans were to fly, they would have to learn to glide first. Some Europeans had tried with so-so results and some fatalities. The Wrights studied the results of those glides, as well as spending hours looking up at gulls and buzzards that wheeled above Kitty Hawk on North Carolina's Outer Banks. It took three years of gliding before they attached an engine to their machine. Others tried power first and did not go anywhere but down. Wilbur and Orville took turns at the controls of the glider, learning to glide and eventually to soar. Their notes were meticulous, and their applications to gliding were painstaking. Finally, in 1903 they were ready with something they called the Flyer, *a powered glider. After many trials, and with Orville at the controls and the tiny engine whirring with all its might, the* Flyer *lifted from the rails and flew 120 feet. Many gliders had done as much, and in fact, the Wrights had gone much further themselves, but no one had ever flown into the wind! Humans were airborne. The cost of the Wrights' four years of experimentation was less than $1,000, one-seventieth the cost of a competitor receiving federal backing.*[2]

While the Wrights actually hid from the media for much of their early years of experimentation for fear that someone might steal their patents, once the patents were secure, they talked more freely. The Wrights also knew how to tell a good story. Shortly before returning to the United States from

France, Wilbur encouraged Orville to release the details of his flight to the media and talk up the story. (It must be pointed out that while the Wrights had little respect for the media, they had great respect for their fellow aviation pioneers and shared a great deal of themselves and their experiments with others. No serious student of flight was turned away from Kitty Hawk or later Huffman Prairie outside Dayton.)[3]

The Wrights' zest for flight, coupled with their zeal and willingness to persist in the face of competition, as well as the weight of history, is a vivid demonstration of the power of discipline.[4]

Involvement, backed by organizational discipline, is a trait that Ann Fudge uses to bring out the best in people. As CEO of Young & Rubicam, a leading advertising agency, as well as a former executive in consumer foods, Fudge understands implicitly that her greatest resource is the people on her team. Creativity is essential. Therefore, she works to bring out the best in her people. "Ideas grow business," Fudge says. "You have to be able to come up with an idea, but you also have to be able to champion an idea—sell it." This belief has enabled her to grow the Maxwell House coffee business into a strong brand, as well as to achieve positions of senior leadership at Kraft Foods.

Fudge pushes herself to be creative. She uses meetings as think-tank sessions, tossing out ideas to see where they end up. For example, she once challenged her team to consider a Kraft product that would be sold only on the Internet. It was merely an example of pushing the envelope. When she worked for Kraft, she said, "I continue to drive for innovation to think of different cereal products, take a different approach." This is an attitude that is vital to an ad agency, where creativity is the currency that makes the firm go. At the same time, Fudge is a realist. All ideas are not equal. Some will soar, others will crash, but the people who offer them must be nurtured. "Even though an idea may not work, [my people] know they won't get beat up." With Fudge, there is a next time. "Here's what we learned, and we're going to carry over to the next initiative we try."

Fudge's early life was shaped by the civil rights movement. As an African-American growing up in Washington, D.C., she experienced racism, but it did not sour her opinion of all people. Today, she manages by inclusion. "Anytime you exclude people, you're taking out the full advantage of what they have to offer." While she values teamwork, she does not coddle; she values independent thinkers and doers. She once told an interviewer, "We hire some very smart people from the very best business schools." But that's not enough. "We stress the importance of teamwork, of working with people."

As a mother and grandmother, Fudge practices the lessons of work/life balance, not an easy task for anyone in a senior leadership position. Like many women professionals, Fudge did not always pursue a linear career path; she put the needs of her family first. That experience, however, deepened her understanding of what it means to lead others; satisfaction at home enables satisfaction on the job.[5] Furthermore, as she revealed to Fortune *magazine, she learned the value of doing a job well before moving ahead. Don't "chart your career path so early on. You're better off demonstrating capabilities at each level." And if you are fortunate enough to have a leader like Ann Fudge, you will get your opportunity to excel if you are willing to put forth the effort.[6]*

$$\text{꧁ ꧂}$$

Discipline is the mettle of execution. As difficult as execution is—and it *is* difficult—it is discipline that keeps execution rolling forward. Discipline requires perseverance. The Wright Brothers spent years studying flight and experimenting with the right designs. Ann Fudge devoted years to honing her skills before rising to the top of her profession. The Wrights applied their discipline to an emerging aviation field; Fudge applies her discipline to getting things done creatively as well as cost-efficiently. Discipline is a trait that successful leaders employ to hold course and keep the execution humming.

WHAT IS DISCIPLINE?

Discipline is not a fashionable word these days. In a culture that worships individualism, we gravitate toward free expression. There is nothing wrong with individualism; it is what makes the free enterprise system work. There also is nothing wrong with free expression; it is a cherished American value. However, individualism and expression have limits within an organization. Belonging to something larger than oneself involves a kind of surrender to the whole. Ideally, the organization, be it a school, a church, a team, a nonprofit, or a business, should serve a kind of greater good so that the individual union with the whole is seen as a contribution to society. Organizations have rules, and you obey them or you leave. It is as simple as that!

Discipline is not compulsion, and in fact, it cannot be. Discipline must come from a sense of free will—*I want to do this!* So let's examine the elements of discipline. The first is *sacrifice*. Whether you want to run a four-minute mile or reduce absenteeism in the workplace, it requires a willingness to exert a degree of rigor. For runners, it means adhering to hours and hours of running long, medium, and short distances and eating right. For managers seeking to bring people to work on time, it means that they too must adhere to the schedule, as well as offer alternatives such as day care, transportation, or "flextime" to people who want to come to work but are faced with personal issues. Likewise, the employees need to embrace the rigor and choose to do it.

A second element of discipline is *perseverance*. Keep on keeping on, as the song says. Perseverance is easy in the end stage of a project when you can see the results. It is harder in the early stages when the project is more visionary than reality based. Leaders need to demonstrate perseverance in their work habits, and they need to drive it home with communication by talking up the virtues of the project and the benefits of the vision.

A third attribute of discipline comes from a sense of *self-lessness*. No agendas, either managerial or personal. What the boss wants or what you want is not what really matters to the enterprise. It is what the customer wants. The customer, of course, is used loosely to mean anyone benefiting from the goods or services offered. When agendas are put aside, discipline is working. This is easy to say and so hard to implement.

Finally, discipline emerges from *commitment*. You must want to do it. As mentioned earlier, discipline is not about forcing people to do something. Yes, it is about adherence to rules and standards, but if compliance is the only course, discipline will never hold. Social service workers are archetypes of commitment. They really live and breathe their mission of social justice, equal opportunity, or health care for the poor. Their commitment sustains them; it nurtures their discipline. Bill Belichick embodies all four attributes by *sacrificing* individual goals for team goals, by *persevering* toward the goal, by putting the *team before self,* and by *committing* to win championships. In this way, Belichick has been able to push the New England Patriots to become the first professional football dynasty of the twenty-first century.

DEVELOP A CULTURE OF ACCOUNTABILITY

Execution rests on a foundation of accountability. For example, when the findings of the *Columbia* shuttle disaster were announced to the public in August 2003, Sean O'Keefe, then NASA's chief administrator, did what too few leaders in public life do: He stood up and took the heat. He made official remarks and made the rounds of the network news shows. His message was direct and straightforward. *We made a mistake, people died as a result, and we will make changes so that it never happens again.* Time will tell if NASA changes, but when O'Keefe was at the helm (he retired in 2004), the agency had a proven leader—one who was accountable.

Contrast O'Keefe's example with that of the many businesspeople and politicians who run and hide at the first sign of bad news. The confluence of catastrophes that hit the United States at the dawn of our new century—corporate scandals, global terrorism, and war—did more than depress the capital markets. These events shattered people's confidence in structures in which they had placed their faith—the stock market, the security agencies, and business and government leaders. Whenever there is a loss of confidence, people want to know why, and so investigations ensue with the purpose of determining who or what was responsible. This reaction is a healthy one, and it rests ultimately on the concept of accountability. Accountability is essential to trust and integral to leadership. Yet, remarkably, accountability seems to be a topic that is overlooked in schools, in sports, and in management. Organizations can do little about what happens outside their spheres of influence, but they can do everything about what happens inside them; therefore, it is essential that managers take the reins on this topic and begin to teach it to their people.

TEACH ACCOUNTABILITY

Teaching takes full advantage of the leadership communication cycle—speaking, listening, and learning. When it comes to accountability, managers need to make it known that accountability matters to them as well as to others. Managers need to listen for consequences, that is, what is happening or what is not happening as a result of their personal actions. And finally, managers must learn from what they have done as well as from what their people tell them. The answers to two questions will determine if you have been accountable: (1) Did you achieve the intended results? and (2) Did you achieve those results through the efforts of your employees, not despite them? Accountability really measures what gets done the right way. For example, say that you are the manager of a marketing team responsible for a new product launch. If you develop and launch the plan successfully and if the product succeeds in the marketplace but in the process you have run roughshod over your people, causing some to quit on you and their teammates, you have succeeded in achieving results but *not* in engendering trust. Accountability measures trust and results.

*   *Make consequences clear.* Most managers know how to set expectations; what they sometimes forget is the consequences of those expectations. In *Hoosiers*, a movie account of the team from a little town in Indiana that won the state basketball tournament, the coach, played by Gene Hackman, establishes a new order on the team at his very first practice. He also makes it clear that if his players play as a team, they will win; if they play as individuals, they will lose. Expectations are linked to outcomes, and that is the essence of accountability.

*   *Develop people to be accountable.* Some managers delegate tasks but not responsibilities. They keep tight reins on the process so that employees become like Pinocchios— all tied up in strings. Yet, when a job goes sour, such managers have no problem cutting the strings and shifting responsibility—in reality, blame—to the employees. Or if the job goes well, the manager is first in line to take credit. You can never expect people to be accountable if you keep pulling strings (as well as yanking chains). Delegation is transference; you assign the job and the responsibility for getting it done. This is how you make people accountable. Groom them for it, and coach them along the way. Sometimes by necessity, typically in crises, employees must leap into the job feet first with

no preparation. This is a good way to learn how to be accountable, but the ride can be harrowing. In such situations, managers need to make themselves available to provide additional resources or at least give support in the form of advice and counsel.

• *Seek solutions not blame.* The best way to nurture accountability is to focus on outcomes. Henry Ford is famously quoted as saying, "Don't find a fault; find a remedy." This is wise counsel from a man whose passion for manufacturing was what we would call today *process improvement.* When people stumble, seek to pick them up, not to stomp on them. Accountability can be cultivated by teaching a better way. The adage about failure being the best teacher is a good one, but all too often managers use failure as an opportunity to push an employee under the bus. Not only is this short-sighted on the manager's part, but it also demonstrates that the manager does not have the wherewithal to manage. By focusing on the outcome, good managers guide their people to good results and do it in ways that develop self-confidence and enable them to take on bigger tasks with greater responsibilities.

DOING IT THE *RIGHT* WAY

Accountability is rooted in ethics and integrity. The ultimate measure of accountability is ethics: Did you do it the right way? If the answer is yes, you have been accountable. If the answer is no, you have not fulfilled both sides of the accountability equation. Accountability means standing up for the consequences. A manager who makes the numbers by fudging figures is guilty of two infractions—cheating and giving bad example to his employees. Likewise, the manager who does not make the numbers but does it honestly and is upfront with his people may be morally upright but may be a poor performer. Accountability addresses the consequences. The first example is fraudulent, for which the punishment should be dismissal; the second example is deficient, for which the sentence should be coaching and, if not successful, removal from management.

While the world is not black or white, the discipline of management is. You either succeed or fail at your objective. But what happens next is where leadership enters the equation. Leaders look at the whole picture. How did the manager succeed? How well did she work with her people? How did circumstances beyond her control affect the final outcome positively or negatively. Leaders must use their judgment to decide consequences. Mandatory sentencing may work for serial murders, but it seldom works in management, save for egregious missteps such as fraud or mistreatment of others.

Accountability is paramount when striving for results, but it is in the striving aspect that managers must insist on doing things right in ways that add to the bottom line, as well as add to the lives of the people for whom they are responsible. This is a major responsibility, of course, but it is what being accountable is all about.

ENERGIZING DISCIPLINE

Communications propel the process of discipline. Stories, particularly heroic stories about men and women who have made sacrifices for the organization, give meaning and honor to the discipline process. And when such stories are told by the leader and by the organization, they give credence to the execution and purpose to the enterprise. For Catholics, the *Lives of the Saints* has stood as a testament to the commitment and passion of their faith. Biographies of saints in personal extremis reinforced the values of the faithful. Readers got an inside look at what the faith meant to the saints and the sacrifices they were willing to make for it. Their personal examples worked to nourish the beliefs of successive generations of the faithful. Saints' lives were vivid examples of discipline in action.

We find another kind of discipline in law enforcement, particularly with homicide detectives. These men and women are possessed by the desire to catch the perpetrator for a combination of different reasons ranging from personal ego to the desire to see justice for the victim and the victim's family. While most murders are open-and-shut cases, thankfully, there are many thousands more that require months and even years of tireless investigation. Detectives do not let go. They work long hours and weekends and give up time with their families in the pursuit of murderers. They sustain themselves with dogged determination and an inner discipline that steels them to go over facts and clues they've seen a hundred times, as well as seek out new leads by interviewing and reinterviewing people again and again. While these investigations can be fulfilling, and the detectives sometimes do receive department and even public recognition, many say that the real reward comes from catching the perpetrators and bringing a form of closure to the victims' families. And it is their personal discipline that keeps them going.

In business, the stakes are not about life and death, although they often affect the livelihoods of individuals, offices, factories, and communities. Manufacturing engineers, the ones who take the products from the laboratory to full production, exert a high degree of discipline. Some of their discipline emerges from the nature of engineering that requires strict protocols and step-by-step processes. Engineers who move into management learn to apply such discipline to striving to meet goals—as all business leaders do. While leading people is not measured in metrics per se, it is measured by achieving intended results that fulfill goals and ideally help the organization and its people grow and develop.

DRIVING DISCIPLINE

Discipline can be acquired. While some of us may have more of it than others, all of us can learn to insist on it as we seek higher goals. There is much a leader can do to inculcate a sense of discipline, and communication plays an essential reinforcement role. A leader achieves discipline by holding people accountable, as well as by coaching and teaching them.

* *Reinforce organizational goals.* Often projects, like tires, lose alignment through excessive wear, not willful neglect. It takes a long time to accomplish a vision, anywhere from three to five years. While initiatives start strongly, they lose steam after a while. It is up to the leader to keep people aligned. Discipline in the form of constant communication can keep people focused on the task at hand. Stories about what has occurred to date in the form of progress reports and obstacles overcome give people a sense that things are moving forward.

* *Insist on ownership.* Too often initiatives lose impetus because of lack of ownership. People do not feel part of the process. It is therefore up to the leader to instill a sense of accountability in all team and department managers. Accountability flows from delegation, as discussed earlier, but it must be reinforced. How? One way is for leaders to meet regularly and ask questions. The questions should not be used to badger but to keep everyone informed and let people know that the leader is engaged. Stories of this kind of engagement further reinforce the organizational vision.

* *Evaluate regularly.* Leaders reinforce accountability by checking for results on a regular basis. Sales organizations are particularly adept at keeping track of sales on a daily, weekly, and monthly basis; manufacturing engineers monitor production and quality on a real-time basis and hold daily meetings to ensure that quality targets are met. Such reporting is a form of communication, of course. Those who work in areas that are less driven by metrics, such as marketing and human resources, can do evaluations

via survey or, better, through informal interviewing. The evaluation again strengthens accountability and also communicates a leader's insistence on discipline.

CONVERSING FOR EXCELLENCE

One of the best ways to ensure discipline in a system is through coaching. So much has been written about coaching that we sometimes overlook what coaching within the management environment really is. It is a conversation between a manager and an employee with the intention of helping the employee arrive at some moment of insight. It produces a degree of self-awareness that the employee can use to improve his performance. Basketball or hockey gives us insight into the process. Watch the head coach on the sidelines. When a player comes onto the bench, the coach invariably will pull him aside and whisper into his ear. The words may range from a rant to a jibe, a bit of advice, or an earful of venom. The purpose is to give the player a heads-up on his play and provide momentary insight into what he can do better.

While game coaching is not a conversation, it opens the door for two-way communication at half-time or after the game. Management coaching should be two-way all the time, although it is entirely appropriate for managers to give advice or encouragement on the fly as a form of feedback. For example, if you notice that your systems engineer is about to enter the wrong data, speak up. Don't wait until the entire system fries.

ONE-ON-ONE LEADERSHIP

Coaching is one-on-one leadership communication. As such, it involves the leadership communication cycle—speaking, listening, and learning. By applying this cycle, you can achieve some positive results.

- *Speak.* Open with a positive. This is critical, especially with new hires. You may be tempted to jump all over someone, but if you do, know this: You will alienate her and turn her off to any benefit that might derive from a constructive conversation. A senior vice president I once worked with excelled in expressing his thoughts verbally and on paper. He made the most of these skills to do a myriad of coaching practices ranging from giving praise to correcting mistakes. His people appreciated his openness and rewarded him with a degree of loyalty that was palpable.

- *Listen.* Listening requires the energy of a sloth on barbiturates but the patience of a crocodile stalking prey. Physically, it requires very little to listen, but it requires a commitment of time and energy to listen with a sense of engagement. You must respond appropriately. Watch Yankee skipper Joe Torre in the dugout; he is as calm as the eye of a hurricane. His demeanor is approachable, and players do approach. He has been able to balance the demands of a meddling boss with the aspirations of a team of high-performers, and he has done it gracefully. Torre is a listener.

- *Learn.* Closing the coaching session is where the learning process begins. Manager and performer come to an agreement about what must be done and when. Marine Corps drill instructors are excellent at gaining agreement with their recruits, but they don't stop at the barking orders; they follow up hours, days, and weeks later to ensure that the lessons ring true. Talk to any Marine, and invariably he will tell you hero stories about his drill instructor; he may have wanted to kill him during basic training, but in the end, the Marine discovered that the instructor had the Marine's best interest at heart.

This speak-listen-learn cycle came alive for me when I watched my daughter's dive coach as he gave instruction to the divers during practice. After each dive, the coach put into words and gestures what the diver did well and what she needed to improve. Then, in later conversation, the coach reiterated key points as the diver demonstrated her technique either on the pool deck or on the diving board. The speak-listen-learn cycle is perpetual and has applications beyond coaching. We all are either speaking, listening, or learning, and we do it at different times of the day with different people.[7]

INVITE FEEDBACK

This cycle also can be applied to you, the manager. Invite your people to give you feedback. It's part of your learning experience. What they tell you will help you to become a more insightful manager and coach. But you cannot expect honest feedback unless you create the right environment. This means that you ask for it and are willing to accept it, especially when it's not what you'd like to hear. None of us likes to hear criticism, but better a few pointed words than a failed project. And don't forget to thank the person who gives you feedback. By doing so, you demonstrate that you appreciate her attentiveness. All this over time generates greater levels of trust, which no manager can do without.

Effective management really is about opening the door for others to achieve. Coaching helps you to open the door into the employee's heart and mind so that you can provide guidance that enables the individual to achieve personal and team goals. This requires a commitment to honesty and authenticity that you nurture by speaking honestly, listening fully, and learning together. It also requires a degree of discipline to repeat the cycle with the individual as well as everyone on the team. The outcome of good coaching is good results, earned by employees who want to excel and have the insight to know how to do it, thanks to their manager-coach.

DISCIPLINED COMMUNICATION

Leaders must exert discipline in their communication. They must do it consistently, frequently, and with constant iteration. Communication requires all the elements of discipline: sacrifice, perseverance, selflessness, and commitment. Stories can bring these characteristics to life. As a leader, when you learn of a man who has set aside his personal agenda for the team, publicize it. When you discover a woman is committed to her cause, celebrate it. Stories provide the texture of discipline and bring it to life. They strip away the sterility of it and imbue it with passion.

Discipline matters because it is what determines whether projects succeed or not. In our age of me-first, discipline is essential to the health of organizations. It involves individual and team sacrifice to be certain, but it teaches valuable lessons that make good execution a repeatable exercise. When people exert good discipline, it rubs off not only on the project but also on the work of others. People begin to see the results, and they want to know what they can do to participate. Discipline is a good antidote to complacency. It is a wake-up call to reality, and it ensures fulfillment of the vision.

Discipline Story Planner

Discipline puts spine into execution and thereby links vision and alignment with results. Consider the following questions to help you insist on discipline. Think of stories to support the discipline process.

- How will you reinforce organizational goals?
- How will you insist on accountability?
- What means will you use to improve organizational performance and effectiveness?
- What steps will you take to ensure that you coach your people? Why will you do this?

Communication Action Steps (Discipline)

- *Aspire.* Emphasize discipline to achieve the vision.
- *Perspire.* Reinforce what discipline entails.
- *Require.* Insist on performance.
- *Transpire.* Reiterate what it will take to succeed.

BILL BELICHICK

As he stands on the sidelines, he appears to be a world apart—cerebral, focused, and observant. Dressed as he is in a nondescript gray hooded sweatshirt, the kind that coaches wore for decades before sweats became fashion statements, he looks almost out of place. You get the feeling that if his face were not so familiar by now, security might swoop down at any moment and cart him away. After all, the sidelines are for players and coaches. Wait a minute, though. He *is* a coach, one of the greatest in the history of the game, and perhaps the best coach in professional football today. He is more Sun-Tzu than Vince Lombardi, more Keynes than Don Shula, more low-key than John Madden. He is Bill Belichick, head coach of the Super Bowl Champion New England Patriots.

It has been said that television is a writer's medium and that film is a director's. If this is the case, the National Football League is a medium made for coaches, but only very special kinds of coaches—ones who know the game thoroughly, can handle the intense workload, and can connect with their players. Today there are two additional elements to coaching in the NFL that add further wrinkles. One is injury. Professional football is a violent game, and players do not last very long. The other is free agency. Here today, gone tomorrow is the modus operandi for many players. Therefore, a head football coach has to be part strategist, part disciplinarian, part recruiter, and part father figure—yes, football is a paternalistic game, unlike any other sport.

Players, no matter how much they may scoff, want to look up to their head coach as the leader. Therefore, the head coach must be a motivational master. And here is where Belichick excels; with so many players coming and going owing to salary restrictions, he has created a team that consists essentially of role players who have come together because they have bought into a system, the New England Patriots system, that blends talent, hard work, and chemistry to produce championships—three Super Bowl titles in the four seasons between 2001 and 2004. In today's professional environment, this is a dynasty.

BORN TO COACH

The man behind the dynasty is himself the son of a football coach. Bill's father was head football coach at the Naval Academy, and young Bill grew up idolizing Navy players such as quarterback Roger Staubach, the 1964 Heisman Trophy winner, who, after his naval service, won Super Bowls for the Dallas Cowboys. Bill's mother said that coaches did not mind having young Bill around. "[H]e wasn't a pest. He was very good at listening and learning and remembering." Bill spent a year in prep school and then attended Wesleyan in Middletown, Connecticut. As reserve defensive end, he had questions: "What if the offense did that?" or "Whose responsibility is that?" He served as team co-captain of the lacrosse team. What he really gained in college was an approach to learning that was both strategic and tactical. "You learn how to think and solve problems," he says. "Here's the problem; you go figure it out." He was an economics major.[8]

Belichick was a good student, but his heart brought him back to his first love—football. His first job was just that—for love. Equipped with his college degree, he volunteered for the Baltimore Colts as an assistant coach in 1975. He performed odd jobs and broke down film, which means taking practice and game films and sorting them into position play and game situations. He certainly earned his keep; by the end of the season, his salary was $50 a week. But he earned far more than a few bucks: He caught the attention of other coaches. "You could see immediately," recalls Tom Marchibroda, then Colts head football coach and something of a legend himself, "that Billy was a hardworking kid."[9] Comments like this have followed Belichick everywhere. Eddie Accorsi, general manager of the Cleveland Browns in the early 1990s, who hired Belichick as head coach, said, "When I sat down with Bill for the first time and he started speaking, you had the feeling that he had been preparing to be a head coach his whole life." Accorsi says today, "I think he is clearly the best coach in the NFL. Everything he does as coach has been planned for. He's at the head of the class, and he's young enough that I don't know where it's going to stop." This was said just prior to the Patriots' third Super Bowl victory under Belichick. That victory gave him 10 victories in postseason play, one more than Vince Lombardi.[10]

It wasn't always this way. For years, like many assistant coaches, Belichick toiled in anonymity. His first head coaching job was with the Cleveland Browns in the 1990s; he took the Browns to the playoffs once but posted a losing record overall and was fired in 1995 after going 5 and 11. It was, however, a learning experience; on reflection, Belichick realized that he tried to do too much. As Damon Hack of the *New York Times* put it, "[H]e did not trust his coaching staff or veteran players to take on leadership roles."[11] For many years—both before and after his first head coaching job—Belichick worked for Bill Parcells, a man known as much for his winning as for his hardedge demeanor. Under Parcells, Belichick was the defensive coordinator, a job he performed well for the New York Giants, helping them to win two Super Bowls. When Parcells later took the New England Patriots to the Super Bowl, Belichick was by his side. Later, Parcells took him back to the Big Apple with the New York Jets and even designated Belichick as his successor. At the last moment, however, Belichick backed out and returned to the Patriots, this time as head coach. Parcells reacted angrily, and the Jets asked for (and received) two draft picks as compensation. Belichick did not look back. Critics note with delight that Parcells has not won a Super Bowl without Belichick, whereas Belichick has garnered three additional ones as head coach. It is the classic example of the pupil topping the teacher.

The job that Belichick has done with the Patriots has earned him the accolades of fellow coaches such as Jimmy Johnson. Johnson, winner of two Super Bowls with the Dallas Cowboys, claims that Belichick's job in 2004 was the "finest job in the history of the NFL." The way he has pieced together his team from free agents is far different from what other NFL coaches faced. Johnson adds, "You can't compare the post–salary cap era to [previous champions]. Back in those days, you had players for six, seven years. You didn't have to cut veterans" because their salaries were too high. Johnson continues, "[D]ealing with new players every year—every week—and still to be of this quality says a lot."[12]

METHOD TO THE SYSTEM

So how does Belichick do it? First and foremost, it is the New England Patriots system that he and Scott Pioli, vice president of player personnel, have developed. "Our overall philosophy is to try to be consistent," says Belichick, "not to do everything and try to have this one big year and the next year we know we're going to pay the price." The secret to team performance is "consistency," and it is evident in training, in film sessions, on the field, and over time. Superstars need not apply at New England. Pioli understands what kinds of players Belichick wants and goes and gets them. A description that many use is "blue-collar-type players," that is, those willing to give you what they have day in and day out. Very important in these days of high-ego, meddlesome owners, the system is endorsed by Robert Kraft, owner of the Patriots. "What I respect about Bill is [that] we have a system in place, and it's not dependent on what the marketplace has to offer." He adds, "It's a system of what players are right for this team." Bingo![13]

The second big reason the Patriots excel is Belichick himself; he is a master strategist. He is a devotee of Sun-Tzu, an ancient Chinese general whose stories comprise the *Art of War*. Sun-Tzu knew how to attack an enemy's strengths as well as his weaknesses. He believed thoroughly in preparation. He also believed in using minimal force or even in avoiding battle all together. Most important, Sun-Tzu was a soldier's general; he believed in taking care of this troops. All these lessons go into Belichick's game plan. It is said by many that he can break down an opponent's strengths and weaknesses and then make those insights accessible to and actionable for his players. Belichick can give his players a list of things to do in a game tactically that enable the entire team to win strategically. This is pure genius. Few coaches can think strategically as well as tactically like Belichick can. With his coaches, he creates game plans that put players into positions where they can succeed.

The third major reason the Patriots win is because Belichick knows how to connect with his people. That connection begins with his two top coaches, Charlie Weis, the offensive coordinator, and Romeo Crenel, the defensive coordinator. The three worked together in one form or another as fellow assistants or reporting to Parcells for more than 15 years. It is a measure of their relationship that both Weis and Crenel were highly recruited as head coaches; one thing holding them back was the Patriots going deep into the postseason every year, so they were not free to take other jobs. That ended in 2005 because other organizations were willing to wait. Weis became the head coach of Notre Dame, and Crenel took over the reins of the Cleveland Browns. In 2005, Belichick added offensive responsibilities to his duties while finding another coach in the New England system to head up defense.

COACH TO PLAYER

Connection extends to players. The players know what Belichick expects both long and short term, and they strive to deliver. In the short term, Belichick helps his coaches develop the game plans that put players in a position to win. "You have to be smart, and you have to study," says linebacker Willie McGinest. "Our game plans relate to what we want to do and what we want to stop [the other team] from doing." Belichick also can be a keen sidelines coach. In the 2004 AFC Championship game, Ted Johnson recalls Belichick giving him "a tip" about the running style of Pittsburgh running back Jerome Bettis. On the next play, the defense stripped the ball from Bettis and returned it 60 yards for a touchdown. It was a play that helped turn the tide and put the Patriots into the Super Bowl for a second straight year. At the same time, the players know that the Patriots expect to compete every year for the Super Bowl. This goal gives the players something big to shoot for and helps to account for the team unity in the off-season when players regularly report for minicamps as well as voluntary workouts. The goal also spurs them to compete harder during the long season.[14]

The system imposes tough decisions. At the start of the 2003 season, the Patriots cut Lawyer Malloy, a defensive back who had contributed to a Super Bowl victory. Another player cut prior to the 2005 was Ty Law, again a key contributor in two Patriots' Super Bowls. The Patriots also released Troy Brown, a likeable and versatile receiver who played cornerback during the 2004 season because the other players were banged up. These cuts were not personal, although some players might think so. As Belichick told the media about cutting Brown, "Nobody has more respect for Troy Brown than I do. I love the kid. He's a good football player, a great leader. . . . He's an inspiration to all of us."[15] A few months later, however, Brown was re-signed without the big bonus.

So, yes, money talks in the Patriots system, but at least the money issue is out in the open; management and players know what they face and why. This attitude is different from that on many other teams, as well as other professional sports; in those situations, obfuscation and cant are more the norm than simple, honest communication. One further example is the contract that Tom Brady signed in 2005; it was for over $60 million, a huge sum indeed, but with three Super Bowls to his credit, he could have garnered far more from another team. Brady's example has a halo effect on the rest of the team; take less, but win together as a team.

FOCUS ON PRIORITIES

Scott Pioli, named the *Sporting News* "NFL executive of the year," backs up Belichick. "Managing success is an organizational thing. . . . People like to put the focus on players too much." This is only part of the team story. Everyone, Pioli states, including coaches and scouts, as well as equipment and video people, realizes that "they're part of the success." Such success feeds off Belichick's energy, his personal will to win—this is what drives him and, by extension, drives the players on his team, knowing full well that "this year's team is going to be somewhat different than the group from the past."[16]

One gets the feeling that Belichick himself really doesn't care what people say about him, but one also gets the feeling that it does do him good when people praise his team, especially when that praise comes from someone in high office, such as the White House. "[W]e're honoring a team that showed a lot of heart," President George W. Bush said in April 2005 when the Pats showed up for a third time two months after their Super Bowl victory. "The commentators would say, 'Well, they are not the flashiest bunch. They are not the fanciest bunch.' They just happen to be the best team. They are a team that showed when you play together, when you serve something greater than yourself, that you win." Belichick took a moment to share something with the president, his trademark gray hooded sweatshirt, and quipped, "As the leader of our country, we want you to be out in front in fashion."[17]

The 2005 season promised to be one that would tax Belichick to the max. After all, he lost some key players like Ty Law at cornerback and Tedy Bruschi at middle linebacker. His two longtime assistants were also gone; Charlie Weis is now head coach of Notre Dame, and Romeo Crenel is head coach of the Cleveland Browns. As of this writing the outcome is unknown, but one thing is certain: Belichick will adapt to change. "I think you have to embrace it because it's inevitable. Change, that's part of it. To ignore it or try to refute it or make time stand still, I think that would be a bigger error. You take what you have and try to make it the best you can, whatever that is." Belichick himself was publicly dismissive of a history-making third consecutive Super Bowl victory, declining comment. Quarterback Tom Brady picked up the challenge. "Everyone knows what the goal is," but he was realistic, noting that the team had yet to play a game. Qualifying for the playoffs focuses the team's attention on the end goal. That attitude is what has enabled Belichick to create a system that is flexible and adaptable, and it has enabled the Patriots to win season after season.[18]

INSIGHTFUL LEADERSHIP

Not surprisingly, Belichick is asked to make what are known in the trade as "motivational speeches." For someone as low key and understated as Belichick, this might seem incongruous. Lombardi used such speeches to lengthen his legend, but in a way, so too does Belichick. At Wesleyan, which granted him an honorary doctorate in May 2005, Belichick revealed that his experience at his alma mater taught him that "we need the ability to change and adapt." He said his concept of leadership was formed in college. "Leadership is about one word: attitude. At the New England Patriots, we talk about attitude, not leadership. That's the energy inside the team."[19] Earlier in the year, Belichick told a group of students at Bryant University in Rhode Island to "Do what you love to do. Go where your passion is, and take it from there." He also elaborated on a consistent theme. "Leadership is not about getting up and giving long speeches. . . . It's about working hard and putting the team first." More insightful, he told them a good story about a player who came to him one training camp asking if the team might get a day off; it was hot, and everyone was spent. Belichick listened and made counteroffer: If the player, a big offensive lineman, could field a punt, then the team would get "a day off." But—and there is always a but in the New England Patriots system—if the player missed the punt, not only would the team practice, but it also would "run 20 laps." It was close; the player nearly dropped the ball, but he hung on. Belichick said, "I never saw a team come together so much than on that one day. . . . There was no moment during the season that the players felt any better than when [that player] caught that punt." And that's a coaching lesson. It is not always what the coach does that matters; it is how the coach responds to the needs of his players. And this is why Belichick is a perennial winner.[20]

Leadership Lessons

- *Set clear expectations.* Everyone on the New England Patriots knows his job. Bill Belichick sees to it that people are informed and are held accountable.

- *Create a system.* In football, as in many organizations, a system of operational principles backed by values will enable individuals to know their roles and how to fit in.

- *Work to win.* Competition is about winning. Bill Belichick puts his players in positions to do what they do best. As a result, the team wins.

(*Continued on next page*)

- *Value consistency*. One of the benefits of a system is that players know what to expect. Belichick strives to manage his team and lead his players in ways that are consistent with expectations, goals, and values.
- *Share the credit*. Players play the game. Belichick always promotes what his players do and, more important, what his team does.
- *Separate work and life*. Bill Belichick connects with his players. He does not, and cannot, allow personal feelings to disrupt the way he coaches his players. It has forced him to cut players he likes personally in favor of doing what is best for the team.
- *Live the values*. Bill Belichick is one of the hardest working coaches. He logs the hours in film and study sessions. His coaches and players follow his lead.

Require

- Risk—how the organization "rolls the dice" (wisely)
- Courage—how individuals keep pushing ahead despite the odds

*F*ulfilling goals is rarely a linear process. It may require boldness, a willingness to take a chance on an emerging opportunity. Such risks must fall within the vision, but they also must be backed by a sense of individual conviction and fortitude we call courage.

CHAPTER 6

"I'm a progressive, collaborative person. I don't want to operate in the old twentieth-century paradigm [of] business vs. labor, the environment vs. business, Democrat vs. Republican. [Most politicians] get so mired in a zero-sum political game that they cannot see what the common goal is. . . .[1]

Governor Jennifer Granholm

RISK

THREE RISK-TAKERS

Idiosyncratic *is not a word typically associated with leaders. By nature, people with idiosyncrasies are self-contradictory and therefore hard to read. For leaders who must bring people together, inconsistencies can be divisive and drive people away from rather than toward a common goal. One entrepreneur (by nature, entrepreneurs are risk-takers) has leveraged his idiosyncrasies to build one of the most powerful companies in sports. Sports icons from Mia Hamm to Bo Jackson and Michael Jordan to Tiger Woods have found a home in this company and thereby have helped to make this company at times the coolest thing in athletic wear. The company is Nike, and it was founded and run for most of its history by one of the quirkiest yet focused entrepreneurs—Phil Knight.*[2]

The roots of Knight's leadership path are found on the track of the University of Oregon, where in the 1950s Knight was a middle-distance runner under the tutelage of the legendary Bill Bowerman. Coach Bowerman was a cross between a Zen master and an old-fashioned tinkerer. He coached running as a discipline and made athletic shoes for his runners. Knight, as well as his teammates, revered him, and when Knight, an accountant by trade, made Bowerman cofounder of Blue Ribbon Sports, the original name for the athletic shoe company, confidence was not in short supply. "Even in the early days," recalls Knight, "when we weren't close to selling $1 million, we thought we would be very competitive in this business. And the thought that we wouldn't be really didn't occur."[3]

In a profile in Fortune *magazine, Knight revealed that he had created a company around his "idiosyncrasies." This trait is not uncommon in mom-and-pop retail operations but can be deadly for a global company. Somehow Knight found a way to make it work, chiefly because he possessed a quality that most entrepreneurs do not have—an ability to delegate responsibility and authority. Knight selects managers and then trusts them to run the company. One company president said that Knight would meet with him "once a week" and later even less.*[4]

With a keen instinct for trends, Knight seized on the athletic boom and contracted with Michael Jordan as a young professional athlete to create a unique brand, Air Jordan. It swept the industry and not only made Jordan wealthy and a household name but also made Nike a powerful force in sports. Yet Knight still had the magic touch with athletes, and he did for Tiger Woods what he had done for Michael Jordan. Nike is now a power in golf apparel and equipment, as it is in basketball. Both Jordan and Woods would have been famous had they never met Knight; it's simply that Knight knew how to leverage their appeal into an iconic brand, a subbrand of Nike.

Not all of Nike's moves have been blessed. In the mid-1980s, Nike missed the shift from sports to aerobics, allowing the much smaller and newer Reebok to come to the fore. Later Nike had to lay off 10 percent of its workforce. And in 1999, there was another downturn. True to form Nike survived each crisis largely owing to Knight's ability to put the right people in place and let them run the business.[5]

Corporate responsibility evolved under Knight at Nike; the company had come under fire for poor working conditions in the developing world and worked to correct them. In Nike's 2005 corporate responsibility report, Knight writes, "After a bumpy original response, for which yours truly was responsible, [Nike] focused on making working conditions better and showing it to the world." Nike's example was hailed by labor leaders, who urged other apparel makers to follow Nike's lead.[6]

As reticent as Knight is as a manager, he is an effective leader. While he confesses to being petrified to speak in front of "more than two people," he knows how to connect when it matters. For example, after taking a leave of absence that coincided with a downturn in Nike's fortunes, he called an all-employee meeting to rally the troops. Attendees found his performance electrifying, worthy of any of the legions of successful basketball coaches that Nike has sponsored. His talk energized the workforce and gave them hope for the future.[7]

Perhaps the secret of Knight is that he understands who he is and what he does well and not so well. He may have gained this self-knowledge from Bowerman. Once when Knight was at Oregon he asked his coach how he could improve his running *time; Bowerman replied, "Triple your speed." This is a piece of Zen wisdom that basically puts the onus of performance, as well as all of the hard work it entails, on the athlete. Knight, by extension, has delegated leadership responsibilities to those he trusts. In January 2005, he gave up the position of CEO to serve as chairman. Of course, his influence will remain at Nike, but his greater legacy may be in creating a culture where people can pursue their passions and achieve a measure of success for themselves as well as for the company they serve. "As an old business professor said to me," Knight says, "the only time you must not fail is the last time you try."[8,9]*

When you think about risk, the image that comes to mind most often is that of a gambler. And when you think of a gambler, you can do no better than Leonard Tose, who once testified before Congress that he had lost upwards of $40 million, maybe more. His losses ranged from a "paltry" $10,000 per evening to multiple nightmare evenings of $1 million losses. When you lose that much, you need to have made that much, and Tose certainly did. And more, much more.[10]

While not exactly a story of rags to riches, Tose built his father's trucking business into a multimillion-dollar enterprise, earning enough to purchase the Philadephia Eagles NFL franchise. Under his ownership, the Eagles made their only appearance in the Super Bowl. He was a strictly hands-off owner; he let his coaches manage. He simply took care of all the financial details and spoiled his players rotten, for which he earned their undying respect.

Tose lived the highlife, but he took many people along for the ride. While he went through four wives, he remained a solid family man—a daughter and two granddaughters eulogized him at his funeral. He was a philanthropist to many—police forces, schools, and religious charities. His favorite coach,

Dick Vermeil, memorialized him by saying, "There's no question he tested life to its extreme. And in some areas he passed with straight A's, and in some areas he struggled a bit. . . . [T]he only person he ever really hurt was himself. He never hurt anybody else. All he did was help others."[11]

As a gambler, he had bad strings—72 nights of consecutive losses. And when quizzed by Congress about gambling, he had one admonishment. "Don't drink when you gamble."[12] This is good advice to anyone willing to take a risk. Maximize your odds by thinking clearly. And know how to tell a tall tale—which Tose certainly knew how to do because he lived them!

There is another kind of gamble that exemplifies what it means to take a risk—a technological leap. The one I am interested in here revolved around a 30-second jump into the air that defied gravity but crystallized a decade's worth of effort. "We had built the better plane. We didn't know whether we would win, but we knew that we should win." Those were the words of Tom Burbage, who headed Lockheed's bid to win the military's next-generation aircraft, the Joint Strike Fighter (JSF).[13]

The acronym JSF sums up what it took to win the contract to build the aircraft—joint purpose of competitors, striking design, and fighting spirit. In essence, Lockheed bet the company on this bid. If the company lost, its days as a military contractor likely were numbered. Lockheed would have to work with competitors (Northrop and BAE [British Aerospace]) to win it. The design was striking because it was focused on the Air Force, which would have the greatest influence on the final product, but tailored as a jump jet for the Marines, which had congressional sway. It took spirit to unite around the project and make it work.[14]

Lockheed did prevail, and when the announcement was made in the autumn of 2001, its manufacturing facility, filled to capacity with workers waiting to hear the news from Washington, exploded in a frenzy of cheers and backslapping.[15] *Lockheed, a decided underdog to rival Boeing, had prevailed. The risk had been worth it, but, in fact, the risk was perfectly reasonable. The company had no other alternative but to do everything possible to win. And it won the right way—with the right product for the right customer and with the right people calling the shots and doing the work.*

This book has marked a progression from vision through results by adhering to ideas and principles inherent to alignment, execution, and discipline. The progression is logical and fulfills its mission, but there is one thing missing—risk! Life itself is neither logical nor always progressive; it is constantly throwing us curves and challenges, as well as providing us with the means to overcome them and in fact become better for them—if we know what to look for. And this is where risk comes in. For Phil Knight, risk is an ongoing challenge from starting a company from scratch to merchandizing major athletes to expanding in new directions. For Leonard Tose, risk was his lifeblood; he loved to bet on sports, as well as on his life. And for Lockheed, risk is an accepted way of doing business with the military. For all three, risk is what you employ to make things happen. On the surface, risk is antithetical to alignment because it means stepping out of bounds.

Risk requires execution, but it involves doing things one's own way to get them done. And finally, risk sometimes is averse to discipline. Discipline involves rigor and adherence to the mission. Risk means taking chances to accomplish a goal. In reality, risk is not about rolling the dice all the time without a care in the world; it's about rolling the dice sometimes and being very careful when you do. How careful? So careful that risk must be tied to vision as well as aligned, executed, and disciplined in order to achieve desired results.

WHY RISK

The American entrepreneurial model is founded on risk. Business leaders grow up on stories about risk-takers. Risk-takers are found in research: Thomas Edison developing the electric light bulb in Menlo Park; John Bardeen, Walter Brattain, and William Shockley inventing the transistor at Bell Labs; and Jim Clark, Alan Kay, and Charles Simonyi pushing various computer frontiers at Xerox. Risk-takers emerge from science: Alexander Fleming isolating penicillin, Maurice Hilleman developing multiple vaccines, and Craig Vetter mapping the human genome. Risk is inherent in business: Steve Jobs and Steve Wozniak laboring in a proverbial Silicon Valley garage, following in the footsteps of two other Silicon Valley pioneers, William Hewlett and David Packard. But risk does not confine itself to small startup ventures. Henry Ford II hired a team of business professionals, nicknamed the "Whiz Kids," from the military and put them to work reorganizing his company to meet the post–World War II boom. Hank McKinnell put Pfizer on an aggressive acquisitions path in order to pursue a "bigger is better" strategy in drug development. What each of these risk-takers has in common is a penchant for something new, something different, and the willingness to pursue it. It's one thing to have an idea; it's another thing to persevere until you develop the electric light or create a whole new business culture.

Entrepreneurs are born risk-takers. They love going against the odds; in fact, the greater the odds, the greater the thrill. Typically, you do not find such people in large organizations. Why? Because all too often risk-taking is discouraged. The penalties for failure overwhelm even the attempts to try. Yet it is necessary to break the model. Successful companies that have stood the test of time, among them General Electric, Kellogg's, and Ford Motor Company, all have taken risks. In fact, each in its own way was built on a less-than-sound business plan. Thomas Edison created a company around his idea for a power grid. William K. Kellogg built a company for health-food faddists. And Henry Ford was a two-time loser; his name-sake company was his third venture. Along the way, each of these companies had to break the mold and start, if not from scratch, then with new and different products. General Electric builds everything from locomotives to jet engines but makes most of its revenue from finance and services. Kellogg's pioneered breakfast cereal and is now a leader in breakfast foods and nutritional products. Ford Motor Company has reinvented itself a couple of times, starting with the development of the moving assembly line and the introduction of blockbuster products including the Model A, the Mustang, and now fuel-efficient hybrid SUVs.

In order to grow, you must take risks. Risks come in all shapes and sizes. They may involve new product innovation, the introduction of a new service model, or a plunge into new drug development. Risks also occur on a department level: adopting a new process model, adapting a new process, or organizing the workflow into cross-functional teams. Risks, of course, are rooted in individuals: what kind of talent to seek, what kind of person to train, whom to promote. Ultimately, risks are personal: Do I take a chance on this, or do I keep on doing the same old thing?

If leaders want to encourage risk-taking, they need to make it safe for people to fail. As discussed earlier, the U.S. Army trains in simulated combat situations as a means to pro-voke mistakes from which it can learn, thus avoiding them in actual combat. Likewise, those of us involved in less lethal enterprises, where people do not die if we make mistakes, need to adopt a similar outlook. The opposite of risk is not failure; the opposite of risk is stasis, or the status quo. Just as change is organic to life, change also is inherent in all organizations. It is necessary to take risks, but to do so appropriately. And one of the best ways to make risk acceptable is to talk about it openly. Conversation brings issues to the surface and allows people a chance to voice an opinion. The manager who wants people to take risks must create a mechanism so that people do not enter risk lightly and, when they do, can find support for both success and failure.

DRIVING RISK

Risk-taking really is a form of execution, the willingness to get things done. The difference is that traditional execution follows established strategies and tactics, whereas risk-taking execution requires either the breaking or abandonment of those strategies and the subsequent adoption of new strategies and tactics. For someone such as Governor Jennifer Granholm, risk is how you rise to power: You risk your career on an election. Communication becomes your tool for bringing voters to your side as you strive to persuade them of the virtues of your ideas, as well as of your ability to execute them if and when you are elected.

- *Assess opportunities and risks.* What else is out there? This is what vision is about, and during achievement of the vision, it is worth asking the question again and again. The "what else" may involve doing something new or holding fast to the current path. It also may involve asking people to do something differently. There is risk in either proposition. By looking first at opportunity, you can ask, "Is it worth it?" This question is easy for entrepreneurs; they may have little to lose. It is hugely powerful for larger institutions. For example, when Pope John XXIII called for the Second Vatican Council, he did so to allow a "fresh wind to blow through." The risks were disaffection and disunity, both of which occurred. Vatican II created waves of change that are still reverberating five decades later. Pope John's aspirations were for a freer, more open, and more genuine experience of faith; its practice resulted in openness to a degree but also a hardening of principles two popes later in John Paul II.

- *Think outside the box.* Many successful leaders look at
  the status quo and wonder why or why not. Formulating
  the question requires guts and the ability to endure the
  smirks and stares of the conventional. Achieving vision is
  a human endeavor and therefore not always linear. Sometimes you have to go backward (relearn things) to go forward. Other times, you need to step out of the box. As a
  means of thinking out of the box, many companies are
  moving to a new kind of innovation model—open innovation—that is, moving innovation from "out of the box"
  to "out of the house." DuPont, for example, is partnering
  with small biotech firms to help it create products.
  Automakers are doing the same with their suppliers.[16]

- *Value creativity.* Leaders who want people to think differently need to establish ground rules that make it okay to
  voice dissent or express contrary opinions. Advertising
  agencies, for example, blend business practice with creative flow. They need both to survive. Their creative
  people live in a world where ideas float in the air; their
  management people live in a world that enables that air
  to keep on flowing in. In other words, they have created a
  viable business proposition for creativity and business to
  flourish together. The result is great advertising that
  delivers great value to clients.

- *Push innovation.* Innovation flows from creativity; it is
  the muscle behind the creative thought. Innovation
  occurs at every level; it is not confined to the laboratory
  or the boardroom. It happens on the shop floor as well as
  at the engineering table. Innovation can be as simple as
  reducing three processes to two or as radical as dropping
  the process entirely but accomplishing the same result.
  Innovation is essential to meeting customer needs, be it
  for service or for new products.

These steps, enriched by appropriate stories, enable a culture of risk-taking to emerge. Rather than being a freelance

operation, though, it is a culture that is enlivened and enhanced by risk and wholly aligned with the vision of the organization and driven by the same commitment to getting things done (execution) on time and within budget (discipline).

VISION AND RISK

When you think about it, a vision is a risk proposition. It takes courage and commitment to go out on the proverbial limb and point out where the organization should go next. However, while the vision may be birthed in risk, what follows in the form of alignment, execution, and discipline is not. As if rediscovering our roots in the vision, we must take risks to see that the vision is fulfilled. It requires men and women at all levels to exemplify the same courage and the same commitment as the leader does. This kind of following really is leadership itself because in doing so these people are bringing other people along, creating successive waves, or generations, of followers. And when the risk is taken, it may be supported with alignment, execution, and discipline. Risk itself propels the vision forward and in so doing supports the entire leadership process.

A very real outcome of risk is failure. Finding blame is blood sport in many companies. When things go wrong, the naysayers love to pull out their fingers, like gunslingers of the Old West, pointing right, left, and center and firing repeatedly, all the while smiling cynically to themselves that they were too smart to make such mistakes. Fat chance! In the aftermath of any failed venture, there is plenty of blame to go around. As John Kennedy noted, "Success has many fathers, but failure is an orphan." And for this reason, people point fingers, insult one another, and move on without making any meaningful change.

If we are honest with ourselves, we will acknowledge that there is something inside of us that wants to find blame; some of us may even take delight in seeing the failures of others. Identifying fault in others does two things. First, it gives us the right to feel self-important, as in "I'd never be that dumb!" Second, it enables us to whistle past the graveyard, as in "There but for the grace of the Almighty go I."

STEPS TO SOLUTIONS

Make no mistake, when things go wrong, you must find the cause. First, determine *what* went wrong; second, find out *why* and *how* it went wrong; and third, identify *who* went wrong. Putting the "what," "why," and "how" before the "who" takes the onus off the individual and puts it squarely where it belongs—on the problem. Communication is essential to avoiding the blame game, and here are some suggestions for rooting out the problems:

- *Delineate the "what."* Before you can find solutions, you need to articulate the problem. The military calls this the *after-action report.* By itemizing the steps, you can define two things: what went wrong and what went right. For example, the new server upgrade software might work fine, but the installation in your system may have been flawed because the technicians were not informed properly about installation procedures. Before you can blame the vendor, you need to isolate the problem by talking to the people involved in the installation process.

- *Address the "why."* Problems in companies do not just happen; they are the results of mistakes by individuals, teams, and organizational structures. Central to the Toyota Production System is the concept of the "Five Whys," a foundation of root-cause analysis that engineers use to discover the causes of problems, not simply their symptoms. Managers can use this concept to find out why things went wrong.

- *Discover the "how."* Answers to the "why" question will sketch a problem, but by asking the "how" question you can get to an immediate cause. For example, if a sales initiative fails to reach its target, answers to "why" may indicate competitive pressures, customer disinclination, or product failure. The "how" will address the process of execution; in other words, perhaps the salespeople did not know how to address competitive pressures, how to demonstrate features and benefits to overcome customer resistance, or how to position product shortcomings.

- *Make it safe to fail.* The root of the blame game is failure. Our culture worships success, and this is good in one way because it gives people something to aim and strive for. By contrast, not succeeding, that is, failing, is judged too harshly. A baseball story illustrates this well: A .300 hitter puts the ball into play 3 out of 10 times, or, to say it another way, he fails to do so 7 out of 10 times. Baseball managers focus on the 3 not the 7, and as a result, .300 hitters are highly valued and well compensated. In the world of manufacturing, Six Sigma, which seeks to limit defects to the sixth decimal point (for example, 3.4 defects per 1 million), looks at reducing failures as a means to an end, not as an end in itself. Six Sigma green and black belts teach others how to leverage lessons learned by failure to improve quality and productivity. Managers can do well to emulate such thinking by making certain that people understand that it is okay to fail as long as they are working within the parameters of the job and doing what they think is best for the team.

- *Look to the bench.* The University of Michigan has won more football games than any other collegiate program. Aside from the fact it has been playing longer than many other universities, it has developed a strong program that promotes those who succeed. Expectations are high not simply for first-stringers but also for second-, third-, and fourth-stringers. When one player graduates or leaves a game owing to injury, seldom does the team lose momentum. Someone is always there to pick up the slack. The coaches use those expectations to motivate players. Managers, too, need to look to develop their talent base so that they will have people ready to step in either full or part time to keep the team rolling. If fear of failure and risk of blame lurk overhead, then talented people will look elsewhere. Again, managers need to make it safe to take risks and acceptable to fail.

- *Put some skin in the game.* If companies are serious about taking risks, they will give their managers a reason to take manageable risks. General Electric, under CEO Jeff Immelt, is pushing to become more innovative. According to Immelt, "[Y]ou're not going to stick around this place and not take bets." Part of executive bonuses will be tied to generation of new ways of doing things. But there is some cushion. As Diane Brady of *BusinessWeek* wrote, "Risking failure is a badge of honor at GE these days."[17]

- *Engage the naysayers.* Some within corporate confines enjoy the blame game. This may be true for any of several reasons: entertainment, boredom, or apathy. Of these, apathy is the greatest sin; it emerges from total disinterest, a disengagement from the business and disenfranchisement from consequences. Thus, instead of pitching in to help, they look for opportunities to pitch rocks. No company can afford such negativity.

Retaliation for attacks may be tempting, but it is short-sighted. Savvy managers, those who know how to get things done the right way, look for their opponents and seek to win them over. Lyndon B. Johnson was a master at winning over his enemies. As he once commented in his less than decorous way, "Better to have 'em inside the tent pissin' out than outside the tent pissin' in." In other words, talk to people who criticize your work. Flatter them by asking for their advice and seek to embrace them as allies. By doing so you gain alternative points of view, which may help to reduce mistakes and also alleviate the blame game. People are far more reticent to criticize something in which they have a stake.

A MANNER OF BLAME

There are occasions when blame must be apportioned and discipline enforced. For example, if the person who made the mistake did so despite warnings from colleagues and bosses, then the penalty must be severe, as in removal from authority. On the other hand, if the mistake was made with the best of intentions and with the support of others, as in the launch of a product that fails, blame can be assigned—but to the team, not to an individual.

Organizations that succeed over time are the ones that have faced adversity and overcome it. In the process, they have had more than their share of incompetent managers as well as organizational screw-ups, but you don't really hear much about them—unless you work inside—because these organizations know how to handle the blame game. They don't play it. They deal with mistakes by finding solutions and teaching their people to anticipate problems, deal with them, and move forward. By removing the stigma of blame from individuals, these companies have been able to stand the test of time.

NET RETURN ON RISK

Failure as it emanates from risk is inherent in leadership. We sometimes need to take chances in order to grow and achieve our potential. As leaders, it is necessary for us to challenge individuals, teams, and the organization as a whole to take risks. Opportunities come to those willing to think creatively and willing to innovate. Stories of risk-takers who succeed become mythic; stories of those who fail become cautionary tales. It falls to the leader to learn to manage risks appropriately. And in this endeavor, communication can reinforce the permissibility of risk-taking, as well as the need to be sensible and in line with vision, mission, values, and culture.

Risk Story Planner

Life is not an orderly process; sometimes you need to take chances in order to succeed. Risk is a means by which you can create and innovate. Consider the following questions to help you think of managing risk. Think of stories to support the risk process.

- How will you assess opportunities for your organization that are aligned with the vision but that were not originally conceived as part of the vision?
- What risks are entailed in striving to fulfill these opportunities?
- How will you encourage your people to think outside the box for both projects and initiatives?
- How will you communicate that creativity is something important to the organization?
- How will you push for innovation?

Communication Action Steps (Risk)

- *Aspire.* Focus on the vision.
- *Perspire.* Find new ways to do things.
- *Require.* Get things done creatively.
- *Transpire.* Push for innovation.

JENNIFER GRANHOLM

If you were to ask the average person to name one thing about the state of Michigan, chances are that he or she would mention that it is the home of the domestic automobile industry. Detroit, Michigan's largest city, is Motown and the cultural, if not geographic, home to General Motors, Ford, and Chrysler. To say that the automobile industry is important to Michigan is like saying that they have oil in Texas. Thus, when the governor of the state actively lobbies to bring Toyota, the archcompetitor to the Big Three, to the state, it's big news. It was not too long ago that anyone driving a foreign car was judged suspiciously.

Today, the lines of what is American or foreign are blurred, the domestic automakers are global, and Asian and European vehicles are manufactured in this country—save for Mazda. Even so, it takes a degree of fortitude, plus a degree of wisdom, to encourage Toyota with tax incentives to expand into Michigan. Prior to this deal, Toyota had a small engineering research facility in Ann Arbor. "Some suggest that the state that's home to the Big Three automakers has a strange role in welcoming Toyota," said Granholm. "But it sends a strong signal that Michigan is open. We want international investment." Such a statement tells you a great deal about the kind of leader that Governor Jennifer Granholm is.[18]

Watching Granholm in action is sport. She's bright, articulate, charming, and very attractive. She's cool under fire and ready with a quip as well as a smile. Teddy Roosevelt spoke of politics as being in "the arena" (the gladiatorial one); Granholm would not disagree, but unlike some pols, she positively seems to enjoy the give and take or rough and tumble of politics. After all, she understands that this is how she will be able to push her agenda and, in her mind, better the state for all constituents. It is not for nothing that she's a graduate of Harvard Law School, where, incidentally, she met her husband, Dennis Mulhern. He decided not to practice law but rather to relocate to his home state of Michigan. So Michigan is where this Canadian-born, naturalized American citizen serves as the state's first woman governor.

AN ACTING STUDENT TURNED POLITICIAN

You can find roots of Granholm's ability to communicate in her training as an actress. On graduating high school, she spent a few years at the American Academy of the Dramatic Arts in Hollywood. And like other aspiring actresses, she found work in theme parks and even on television, as a participant in the *Dating Game*. Los Angeles was not for her, however, and she won a scholarship to the University of California at Berkeley, where she majored in French and political science. She then matriculated to Harvard Law School. Both schools sharpened her politician acumen. While at Berkeley she spent her junior year abroad in France and became involved in helping Soviet Jews emigrate. At Harvard Law she edited the *Civil Rights and Civil Liberties Law Review.* She also supported the Mondale Ferraro bid for the presidency in 1984.[19]

After arriving in Michigan, she clerked for a judge but later found her place as corporate counsel in the office of Ed McNamara, long-time chief executive of Wayne County. McNamara took a liking to the energetic Granholm, calling her a "child of destiny." In 1998, she ran for and won the job of attorney general, becoming the state's highest-ranking Democrat. As attorney general, she pushed the state to develop a new "high-tech crime lab," and she successfully prosecuted online purveyors of a "date rape drug," as well as of child pornography. She also elevated her name recognition so that in 2002 she was perfectly poised to run for the state's top job.[20]

First, however, she had to run against a couple of well-known Democrats in the primary—one, a former governor; the other, a former Democratic whip in the U.S. House of Representatives. Neither helped his cause by bashing her more than they advocated their own proposals. You got the feeling watching the primary that these two old pols couldn't stand being upstaged by someone not only more attractive but also more articulate than they were. She beat both handily and faced Dick Posthumus, a Republican, in the election. Well known in political circles but not well known statewide, Posthumus ran a diligent campaign; he was focused and well organized, but as one Republican operative lamented, "If we talk about the issues, we'll win. If it's about rock stars, we won't." This last comment was in reference to Granholm's good looks and star appeal. Granholm won a tight race, thanks in part to a big turnout in the city of Detroit, a noted Democratic stronghold.[21]

Granholm campaigned as a new-style politician, one who wanted to work with all elements of government not as an adversary but as a collaborator. In her acceptance speech to the Democratic convention, she had made a reference to Abraham Maslow's "hierarchy of needs." The state apparatus she was taking over had plenty of needs and plenty of hierarchy, but not in ways that Dr. Maslow would advocate. The state was in debt and had entrenched interests in education, local government, and business. Granholm did not back down. Ever the communicator, she did not mince words. After less than two months in office, she said, "I need everyone to understand the seriousness of the state budget crisis," whereupon she released a budget calling for cuts of upward of $150 million. This was not an auspicious start, but it was a straightforward one.

CHALLENGES OF GOVERNING

Michigan, like many states in the Upper Midwest, is subject to periodic downturns in the economy. With every downturn, there are fears that this crisis may be fatal, crippling the state's manufacturing base so severely that it would never be able recover. While the state has always rebounded in the past, the post 9/11 downturn not only has crimped business, but it also has hurt state and local governments so that many municipalities have had to close schools and lay off police, fire, and emergency workers. All this hits the governor's office. Reviewing Granholm's public comments for the past few years gives one a taste of the range of issues a governor faces. One recalls the adage that Tip

O'Neill, long-time Speaker of the House of Representatives, used to his advantage: "All politics is local."

Jobs are a major concern. In 2005, Granholm's administration proposed a job-development package for 40,000 new jobs in such fields as "construction, architecture, engineering, [and] consulting." According to Granholm, "This is a plan to create new opportunities for economic development around the state that will put shovels in the ground and paychecks in workers' pockets." Critics are skeptical that it's a make-work plan. To counter such fallout, Granholm took her message on the road, leveraging her ability to size up a problem and its solution in terms that constituents can understand readily.[22] In a speech before the Detroit Economic Club, when she stated that the global economy was one of "eat or be eaten," Granholm added, "I for one refuse to allow Michigan to become another country's meal."[23] A few days later she added to that thought: "We must think big, nothing small. We must jump ahead not just of other states, but of other countries, or we will be left behind." Another job plan includes a $2 billion bond issue to raise funds for life sciences, alternative energy, and new automotive technologies.[24] Clearly, this is a politician who knows how to relate to a state that has been on the backside of globalization.

Michigan's challenge is to attract new employers. One way to get companies to locate in Michigan is to offer an educated workforce. Education is a declared priority for Granholm, and she's developing the issue in a number of ways. For example, Granholm advocates a stipend of $4,000 to be paid to all students who finish two years of post–high school education, including college or technical school. This plan would supplant a $2,500 grant given to students who score highly on an achievement test administered in high school. Granholm says that her plan "puts the incentive where we think the economy demands it to be, which is the completion of college, not completion of a test." Qualification for this award also will depend on the completion of 40 hours of community service during high school. It is Granholm's way of helping to instill "an ethos" of service in young people.[25] Furthermore, she says, "It's important to help open the door . . . to a college education. . . . We don't want to ask people to sign up for a bunch of student loans under the promise that we someday may help pay them."[26]

Granholm also challenges parents to play a role. During that same speech to the Detroit Economic Club that was described by the *Detroit News* as "fiery" and in which she called herself an "optimist," she demonstrated the passion of her convictions. In reference to a poll, Granholm said, "Three-quarters of Michigan residents do not believe it's essential for their children to go to college. That's mind-numbing. Parents need to believe it's essential." She also cited a statistic stating that only 3 to 5 percent of parents view engineering and information technology (IT) viable options for their children, "Wake up! That's a clear indication that we have a mind-set to change. . . . Every child in Michigan must go to college."[27] She also urged parents to limit the time their children spent watching television and playing electronic games.[28]

Granholm is an out-of-the-box thinker, too. One example is her encouragement of the consolidation of small school districts. By bundling resources, districts can reduce administrative and service costs and focus scarce resources on education. Her administration is also working with the state's major research-oriented universities, including the University of Michigan, Michigan State, and Wayne State, to promote Life Sciences, a comprehensive initiative designed to develop and pioneer next-generation health care applications and therapies.[29]

Granholm also wants to push Michigan to the forefront of research into alternative energy. This interest couples with the state's automobile industry. But Granholm likes to look beyond the next hill. As she told the *Detroit Free Press* in reference to a statistic she is fond of quoting, "[T]hat says 75 percent of the companies on the Fortune 500 in the year 2020 don't even exist today." If Michigan wants to be a player in creating and developing tomorrow's businesses, it must do so with the realization that it will require "technology and forward thinking and university partnerships."[30]

PEOPLE MATTER

Along the way, Granholm has found ways to address the human side of government. Her husband, Dan Mulhern, is a leadership consultant, and he helped develop a vision-and-values initiative for state employees. It focuses on "excellence, teamwork, integrity, and inclusion." It is nothing earth-shattering, but according to Mulhern it is a way to make Michigan "a great work culture." In doing this, it would enable the state government to be more responsive to citizens' needs. Mulhern also serves as an unpaid adviser to the governor and occasionally as a speechwriter. He does something else; he has assumed primary care of the couple's three children, a factor that male state governors are never queried on but which their female counterparts are. With Mulhern, one gets the feeling that Granholm has a soul mate and full partner, one who has put aside his career for the moment to serve her commitment to public service.[31]

When Granholm was asked by the editorial board of the *Detroit Free Press* to discuss her vision for the future, assuming that she is elected for a second term in 2006, she replied that she wanted Michigan to be known as a leader in alternative energy and thereby attract people to the state. She also wanted "racial polarity" to end and wanted Detroit to gain in population, reversing a decades-long decline. Mass transit for southeast Michigan is another desire; after all, Detroit is Motown. All in all, Granholm is an independent thinker, but one who is able to elevate her ideas through her communication and thereby make them accessible to debate. Being a governor is a very different proposition from running a corporation, of course. Governors have power, but most of their accomplishments come by working collaboratively with the legislature and marshalling the support of independent interests. This is not an easy job, but it is one that requires what Granholm is good at—connecting with people honestly and authentically.

Plenty of pundits have prognosticated that Granholm has the kind of appeal that can translate into national office. However, as a Canadian-born naturalized American citizen, the governorship is the highest executive elective office to which she can aspire. For now, the state of Michigan, with its myriad problems and commensurate opportunities, captures her full-time commitment. With her drive, dedication to public service, and ability to articulate the issues simply, forcefully, and with conviction, the rest of Granholm's story is yet to be written.

Leadership Lessons

- *Think outside the box.* The apparatus of government moves slowly. Sometimes it benefits from a "fresh eyes" approach to problem solving. Jennifer Granholm provides those eyes, as well as some good ideas.
- *Communicate regularly.* All politicians can speak. Granholm can connect. She frames her messages in ways that ring true to her constituents. She blends policy with people in order to make her ideas palatable.
- *Take the heat.* It was Harry Truman who said that if you can't stand the heat, stay out of the kitchen. Governing the state of Michigan in an economic down cycle raises the temperature of every issue, every bill, every debate. Granholm can give and take with the best of them.
- *Demonstrate conviction.* If you want people to follow, you need to demonstrate that you are committed. Granholm is an ardent speaker and displays the

(*Continued on next page*)

passion of her beliefs on issues such as the economy, jobs, and education.

- *Balance work and life.* Few men in powerful positions are expected to care for their children. Women, even governors, are. Granholm has balanced the needs of the people with the needs of her family. (The support of her spouse has made it possible.)

- *Instill hope.* It is human nature to look on the dark side, especially when it comes to government. Granholm projects a positive force of energy that gives her message a lift and her policies some pizzazz.

C H A P T E R

"There is only one thing that we can claim with complete confidence is indispensable to courage, that must always be present for courage to exist: fear. You must be afraid to have courage."[1]

Senator John McCain with Mark Salter
Why Courage Matters

COURAGE

VOICES FOR COURAGE

Working as a business journalist is typically not considered dangerous business; such journalists may have to endure the barbs of self-inflated executives who do not like to read anything but positives about themselves in the media. There is an exception, however, and that is Russia. There the barbs

147

come in the form of bullets, especially when journalists get too close to the truth when reporting on the nefarious lives of the looters of public trust and (formerly) public coffers disguised as modern businesses. This was the world into which Paul Klebnikov entered and from which he did not return. He was gunned down outside his office in Moscow in the summer of 2004 at age 41, the fifteenth journalist killed in the line of duty in Russia since 2000.

Described as a man with wide-ranging interests, Klebnikov was, above all, courageous. He went to Russia fully aware of the risks and hazards of business reporting. His heritage is thoroughly Russian; in fact, his great-grandfather was an admiral serving in the White Russian navy when he was assassinated by the Bolsheviks during the Russian Revolution, and another ancestor was exiled to Siberia in 1825 for anticzarist activities. Klebnikov was born and raised in the United States, and he took a doctorate at the London School of Economics.[2]

Klebnikov's story on Boris Berezovsky, described as the wealthiest of the Russian oligarchs, earned him the enmity of a dangerous foe, a man who, despite his business interests, also was a member of his nation's Security Council.[3] Power and corruption go hand in hand, a fact that Klebnikov understood instinctively and did not hesitate to investigate.

After reporting on the country for years, Klebnikov became the founding editor of Forbes Russia, *which meant that his voice would be heard not just in the West, as it had previously, but also in Russia and in the Russian language. As his editor, Steve Forbes, put it, Klebnikov saw Russia not just as a land of oligarchs but as "entering an era in which a lawful, innovative, opportunity-enhancing, free-enterprise kind of capitalism was beginning to emerge."[4] Klebnikov's reporting would help move this new revolution forward. Sadly, his goals ran smack into the now-entrenched counterrevolution of corruption. Reporters are routinely beaten or intimidated; no one has been brought to justice for the killing of Klebnikov, nor any other journalist, and so Russia remains a dangerous beat for anyone desiring to speak the truth about business practices.*

In addition to his reporting for Forbes, *Klebnikov wrote books, one featuring Berezovsky, as well as other Russian bandit oligarchs. His final book also demonstrated courage of another sort;* A Conversation with the Barbarian *was "an appeal to Europeans to defend Christian civilization against Islamic extremism." Extremists, like oligarchs, do not like to be challenged. The Chechen man featured in the book did not like how he was portrayed and, according to a Russian prosecutor, ordered Klebnikov's death, which was carried out by a Chechen criminal gang. A warrant for the Chechen's arrest was issued in June 2005, nearly a year after the assassination.*[5]

Although Klebnikov was an American, The Economist *closed its obituary this way: "His death is Russia's loss."*[6] *This statement sums up Klebnikov's commitment to the American ideals of freedom and public trust and his life-long commitment to his ancestral homeland. Steve Forbes, closed his personal tribute to Klebnikov by writing, "Paul passionately believed in this better Russia and felt his work would play a role in moving this redemptive process forward."*[7]

One of the tragedies of war is that it's always the innocents who seem to suffer the most. The only thing sadder than this cliché is that it happens to be true. Take the case of Marla Ruzicka, a 28-year-old aid worker. Ruzicka had gone to Iraq to help the innocent victims of war; she herself ending up becoming a victim in April 2005 when she was killed on her way to the Baghdad airport along with her long-time aide. She was on her way to check on the status of a child.

With her youthful California-style looks and irrepressible smile—not too different from actress Renée Zellweger—Ruzicka looked far too young to be caught up in the horror of war. She looked as if she might be more at home on a college campus or, better yet, at spring break. Yet Ruzicka had a passion to help the needy that transcended any desire to put herself first.

Ruzicka was one smart and savvy activist. She told the New York Times *that she had attended a Senate hearing in 2002 where Secretary of Defense Donald Rumsfeld was testifying. "I didn't scream. I thanked him for testifying. And I started talking about civilian casualties." With that kind of candor and disarming manner, Ruzicka was able to pry information from all kinds of sources, military and civilian. Her mission was to put a face to numbers, as she commented for a television news report that ran on PBS* NewsHour *after her death.*[8]

She got her first taste of war in Afghanistan and later moved to Iraq. She identified victims of warfare and sought ways to help them. Her modus operandi was to go into the field where casualties had occurred, interview survivors to determine responsibility, and then seek compensation for them if the U.S. forces had been involved. She was not seeking to point fingers—after all, our military goes to extraordinary means to avoid civilian casualties—but to get reparations. "I'd rarely met someone who could combine such strident activism with canny politics," says reporter Vivienne Walt of Time. *Ruzicka parlayed her talent to chat up journalists as well as military, governmental, and health care officials. Anyone who might help her cause was subject to her charms. In 2004, she founded CIVIC (Campaign for Civilian Innocent Victims in Iraq) to identify Iraqis who had fallen victim to war and to seek compensation from the U.S. government. To the amazement of many, she succeeded in wresting $17.5 million in foreign aid.*[9]

Her compassion was genuine, evident not only in words but also in gesture. Video footage of her shows her reaching out to touch a woman who suffered a loss or to take the hand of a toddler or cause a child's face to break into a smile. It is easy to see why she succeeded; who could say no to her? In a final e-mail to her friend, CNN journalist Peter Bergen, she wrote, "We are helping lots of kids with medical care—this place continues to break my heart—need to get out of here—but hard." Her last words, according to an Army medic who arrived on the scene of the car bombing, were, "I'm alive." Sadly, not for very long. Yet the outpouring of concern generated by the news coverage of her death guarantees, at least for a little while, that her cause will live on. And most especially her memory will live on in the hundreds, if not thousands, of civilians she helped. The story of Marla Ruzicka remains one of hope—the hope that one person did make a positive difference.[10]

⋘⊙ ⊙⋙

No discussion of courage can overlook a man who sacrificed his career for his ideals. John Boyd was a fighter pilot—pugnacious, confident, and absolutely committed to his own point of view. He also was educated in engineering, and as Robert Coram illustrates in his biography, Boyd, *he could articulate the engineering side of aerial warfare. Sadly, it was his legacy of confrontation that caused him to remain a colonel when he should have been a general. As a fighter pilot in the time of bomber warfare, led by none other than General Curtis LeMay, the architect of carpet bombing in World War II, Boyd was an oppositional figure. His argumentativeness did not complement his chances for promotion.*

Granted, Boyd's ego was monumental. His claim to fame was that he could jump any fighter pilot in a dogfight. As the lead plane, he would be tailed; with a series of quick maneuvers, he could turn to pursuer and have the former in his gun sites. Only one fighter ever tied him; the rest were defeated. Boyd also was a good instructor and teacher; although gruff, he could be gracious and understanding, as with the case of First Lieutenant Ron Catton, who was on the verge of being thrown out of the Fighter Weapons School, the most prestigious school for fighter pilots. He issued a challenge to Catton, saying that no one had ever made it through with a series of 100s. Catton rose to the challenge and later became an instructor.

Boyd's major contributions to aerial warfare were simplification and quantification. By reducing his own skillful and intuitive maneuvers to rules, he formulated a warfare handbook. He later sought to simplify it by applying formulas derived from math and physics. According to Coram, Boyd was a remarkable briefer. He balanced his mastery of the subject matter with a passionate energy. He would dance around the stage with energy as he told his story.

His greatest aeronautical briefing and the one that changed fighter designs was the E-M (energy and maneuverability) briefing. Through physics and math, backed by air tests, he was able to prove that every single U.S. fighter was inferior to a MiG; it was a stunning revelation, one that rocked the Air Force. Fortunately, Boyd was not only able to diagnose; he could also teach pilots how to maneuver in dogfights and save themselves. Boyd was able to sway General Walter Sweeney, head of Tactical Air Command, to make necessary changes. Boyd also shared his findings with aircraft makers.

Boyd's greatest contribution may be his "Patterns of Conflict" briefing, in which he traced the history of warfare and made the case for a more nimble fighting force, that is, maneuver warfare. This briefing took five hours to deliver but could have lasted much longer. It synthesized his thoughts on warfare. From it, others extrapolated the theory of fourth-generation warfare, hand-to-hand combat in cities where the enemy is intertwined with the citizenry, as we saw in Somalia in 1993 and in Iraq after the invasion of 2003.

From the "Patterns of Conflict" briefing emerged the OODA loop, which today is taught to fighter pilots. It is really a decision-and-review cycle, but it can be practiced one step at a time as observe, orient, decide, and act. On a broader scale, it encompasses much more: "observe" includes strengths, weak-

nesses, opportunities, and threats (SWOT) analysis; "orient" involves placing observations in context; "decide" involves decision making; and "action" is following through.

Many people believe that Boyd himself never received the recognition he deserved for his contributions. He easily could have become a general had he been more politic in his demeanor, but that was not his style. Even after leaving the Air Force, he refused most remuneration for government contract work, thinking that since he was on a military pension, it would be greedy to "double dip." Boyd sacrificed his own comfort, and tragically his family's financial security, to pursue his ambitions as well as his ideas. A maverick's maverick, he died something of a broken man in terms of health, but unbroken in spirit and commitment to his ideals.[11]

ɩ❧

Courage is vital to leadership results. Paul Klebnikov believed that as an editor of a business publication, he could help usher in an era of economic freedom for his ancestral homeland. Marla Ruzicka put herself on the line to help those disenfranchised by war. And John Boyd sacrificed his career for ideas he believed would improve our nation's defense. All these actions demanded courage. And it requires courage to exert discipline and hold to execution, especially when forces both human and economic are pushing you to take the path of lesser resistance. Middle managers feel this push constantly. They are pushed by their superiors to install a new process or achieve a high quota, yet they may not often have the resources to pull it off. Their direct reports push back because they are overworked and over-stressed, not to mention feeling underpaid. It falls to the manager, then, to stand up to her bosses and ask for more in terms of resources and personnel. No manager likes to plead such a case; it takes guts, pure and simple, to stand up for yourself and your team.

COURAGE EMPOWERS RISK

Courage is essential to risk-taking. Few of us would take a chance if we did not have some ounce of courage inside pushing us forward. As discussed earlier, the secret of good risk-taking is information and intelligence, that is, knowing the odds and acting when they are favorable to you. Still, it requires strength of conviction to move ahead. Without courage, we would all live in the status quo.

One man who combined courage with discipline, execution, and risk is Ed Breen. He had the unenviable task of succeeding Dennis Kozlowski, the deposed chief of Tyco, who had exited under a cloud as well as a flurry of subsequent indictments for corporate malfeasance. (Kozlowski was convicted in June 2005.) So corrupt was the culture at Tyco that Breen would have to clean house, starting with the board of directors. "There was no way I could have backed down. If we didn't replace the board, we wouldn't have been able to proceed." The purge rolled corporate-wide. In 2004, there were fewer than 12 employees left of the 300 who were there when Breen came aboard in 2002. But Breen did more than cut; he sought to add value to the enterprise, transforming Tyco into less of a holding company and more of a "world-class operating company." Part of this process called for more investment in research and development to grow "organically" rather than simply by acquisition. Revenues for 2004 were up 12 percent to over $40 billion. This was risk-taking, yes, but one with a degree of courage.[12]

ACTS OF COURAGE

We have been witness to some inspiring forms of courage in recent years: the firefighters at the World Trade Center, our troops in Afghanistan and Iraq, and closer to home, two women who dared blow the whistle on their organizations, Sherryl Watkins of Enron and Colleen Rowley of the FBI. Both women wrote memos to their bosses revealing deep troubles within their organizations. We have heroes in our midst but not enough so as to forget what they do nor to cultivate the characteristics that breed them. Every organization needs men and women willing to stand up for what they believe in; often that takes courage. Communicating what courage is and why it makes a difference is essential to the health of an organization.

- *Value courage.* Managers can make it known that they respect people who stand up for their convictions, especially in the face of the odds. While the lubrication that enables organizations to perform is conformity, too much conformity leads to groupthink; people do not express views outside the norm either because they are afraid or because over time they forget their value. Managers have to encourage a degree of dissent in order to validate ideas. If employees are shaking their heads at everything their managers say, the same old results will repeat themselves. It takes a degree of courage to express a different point of view, but managers should foster this as a means of strengthening the thinking process and of engendering team collaboration.

- *Publicize courage.* The military honors those who serve in dangerous situations, and the act of giving a medal accomplishes two things: (1) It honors the recipient for valor, and (2) it communicates to others that courage under fire is commendable. Police, fire, and rescue departments follow this example. While few things in management within the corporate sector are hazardous, senior leaders can make it a point to recognize people who stand up for their convictions in the face of the odds in order to achieve desired results.

- *Tell stories of courage.* As part of a leadership development program for a major industrial concern, participants, all of whom were middle managers or above, were asked to talk about examples from their careers about when they had witnessed examples of courage. The discussion also brought up examples of when managers did not exert a measure of courage about decisions, people, or policies. The discussion was enriching for its honesty, and participants came away with new understandings of their role as leaders.

COURAGE TO POSTPONE

As critical as courage of convictions is, sometimes it takes greater courage to take a step back for the good of the team. Suppose that you are working on a project in which you have invested many months and much energy. Then you get word that departmental budget cuts are coming. If you put aside your project, the rest of the department can survive. It is not life or death, but it is very hard to make this choice. Rather than kick and scream, therefore, perhaps it might be better to accept your fate so that others can still have a job. Managers face this kind of conundrum every day. Painful as it is, however, sometimes you can gain greater esteem from personal sacrifice than from personal excellence.

Two explorers of the Antarctic, Ann Bancroft and Liv Arnesen, learned that it is acceptable to say no to the next challenge. Their goal was to be the first women team to trek across the Antarctic. They endured untold hardships in the form of blizzards, extreme cold, and frequent slips and falls, not to mention pulling hundreds of pounds of gear across 1,700 miles of icescape. As they neared the end, though, they realized that they did not have enough time to finish the journey before the Antarctic summer would end, so with great reluctance they called their crew and asked to be rescued. Three years of planning and training had come to this crashing end, and their crew tried to dissuade them. However, as Bancroft put it later, "For me, exploration is about the journey to the interior, into your own heart. I'm always wondering, how will I act at my moment of truth?" Both she and Arnesen proved themselves nobly.[13]

COPING WITH FEAR

John McCain, himself no stranger to acts of courage after having spent five and a half years as a POW in North Vietnam, advises that courage is not all about making the right choices. It is about understanding your own limitations. Fear plays a significant role. "Courage is not the absence of fear, but the capacity to act despite our fears."[14] Sometimes the greatest acts of courage occur not when the bullets are flying, nor the fires raging, but when individuals step forward to raise questions about the direction their company has taken. Whistleblowers are a prime example. While some who blow the whistle may do so out of spite or revenge for not being promoted, many others do so out of a personal mission. They have discovered malfeasance or fraud in their companies and feel compelled to do something about it. You also will find courage in employees who have the guts to confront a bully boss, one who is making life miserable for fellow employees. By taking a stand, they may risk their opportunities for advancement or even their chances of being retained. Yet they do it because they feel that it is the right thing to do. There is fear, yes, but their inner fortitude prevails.

COURAGE PROLIFERATES

Images of courage abound—soldiers fighting in the field, police patrolling the streets, firefighters hosing down burning buildings, and school teachers battling poverty and ignorance. You find these examples in the headlines or on television, but you also can find other examples sitting next to you every day in the workplace. There are single mothers who never miss a day of work, all the while ensuring that their children are fed, sheltered, educated, and most of all, loved. There are men at work dealing with aging parents who need their attention and their resources, often at the expense of work activities. And there are men and women at work battling personal demons such as addictions to cigarettes, alcohol, or gambling to which they do not succumb but rather fight against daily. Courage is all around us. All we have to do is look and be thankful for people who possess it, for our world is a better place for them. Courage is a virtue, and we are blessed by all who practice it.

Courage Story Planner

Courage is the capacity to act on our convictions. It may be strong in some instances and weak in others; courage demands that we know when to exert it against the odds. Think of stories to support examples of courage.

- How will you value courage?
- How will you publicize courage?
- What stories will you tell to promote courage?
- How can you make it safe for people to express their workplace fears?
- How will you sustain courage? What will you need to do to focus people on the courage required to execute the strategies of your vision?

Communication Action Steps (Courage)

- *Aspire.* How do we value courage?
- *Perspire.* What did we do to demonstrate courage?
- *Require.* What kind of courage will it take to overcome roadblocks?
- *Transpire.* How have we pushed ourselves to exert courage?

JOHN MCCAIN

Perhaps the moment will not mean much in the course of his life; it may not even be a footnote after all that he has accomplished.

He is a graduate of the U.S. Naval Academy, a former Navy pilot, and a long-service U.S. senator from Arizona. For many Americans, however, their perception of his life is colored by the five and a half long years he spent as a North Vietnamese prisoner of war in the infamous "Hanoi Hilton." He was beaten and berated, taunted and tortured, and through it all he, along with his fellow POWs, persevered. Thus, when the interviewer, Chris Matthews, a tough-minded television journalist-pundit but outspoken admirer, asked him what he thought of Jane Fonda, his reaction was so low key that it immediately punctured perception and got to the heart of the matter. He is John McCain, and here is what he said about Jane Fonda, who had traveled to North Vietnam while he was imprisoned there and was photographed sitting on an antiaircraft gun, the kind that was pointed at the skies where U.S. pilots flew: "[I]f anyone regrets something they have done—I've regretted some of the things I've done in my life—that's fine with me." A moment later he added, "Look, I didn't like it. I don't like it. But for me to hold a grudge against her . . . it's a waste of time." When Matthews played the clip of McCain for Fonda on his next night's show, she seemed visibly moved. Whatever she thought was immaterial because John McCain had moved on, as he has been moving on for his entire life.[15]

So popular is McCain that reports of him joining friend and fellow Vietnam vet John Kerry as vice presidential candidate in the 2004 election became a major news story. The more McCain denied it, as he had denied reports of running as an independent in previous elections, the more the story seemed to gather momentum. Of course, it never came to pass, but the story is indicative of the esteem in which McCain is held by people of both parties. Popularity polls for future presidential contenders show him high on the list. More impressive is that he, along with statesmen such as Colin Powell, rank high in attributes such as respect and trust. Of course, popularity polls are like beauty contests—ephemeral. McCain the man, however, is anything but.

IN CAPTIVITY

McCain's esteem is well founded. Son and grandson of career naval officers, McCain grew up a Navy brat and lived for some time in Washington. He was accepted to Annapolis, where he studied without distinction. On graduation, he qualified to become a Navy pilot and eventually ended up flying an A-4 jet over North Vietnam. On October 26, 1967, a surface-to-air missile (SAM) hit his wing, and as McCain writes, in pilot's parlance, "I was killed." The subsequent ejection knocked him out cold and also broke both arms and a knee. He landed in a lake during the middle of the day and was captured immediately, beginning an odyssey that would transform him from hot-shot aviator to prisoner to war hero—not an appellation he applies to himself. Reading his account of his long sojourn, the reader is struck by the sheer brutality that the POWs were subjected to—certainly the North Vietnamese did not adhere to the Geneva Convention— as well as the deprivation. McCain was kept in solitary confinement for two years. Communication was forbidden. Of course, the guys got around that; they developed a system of hand signals, as well as a system of tapping, a kind of Morse code, to indicate letters of the alphabet to spell words. It was slow and laborious, but it kept the men in tune with one another. As McCain put it later, "I had a nearly devout belief in the restorative power of communications."[16]

McCain had one advantage that the other prisoners did not: His father was a high-ranking admiral, and the North Vietnamese knew it. McCain received rudimentary care for his wounds as a result of that family connection. However, that same connection was turned against McCain when his captors offered him early release. This would put McCain in an awkward position, because the POWs had a code of honor; releases were fine as long as the longest-serving prisoner was released first. This did not happen, but some prisoners were released, which the North Vietnamese turned into propaganda victories. McCain was urged by his fellow prisoners to accept his early release; after all, he had serious wounds from which he had not recovered fully. McCain refused three times; on the day of his third refusal, July 4, 1968, his father, Admiral John McCain, was promoted to Commander in Chief of the Pacific, something that McCain did not learn about until later. At the completion of the Paris peace talks, the POWs were returned home. McCain went through corrective surgeries, as well as intensive physical therapy. He concludes *Faith of My Fathers* with a reflection that "Vietnam did not answer all of life's questions, but it answered many of the most important ones."[17]

CLIMBING THE POLITICAL LADDER

McCain returned to active duty but could not fly again; he ended up working in Washington as a military aide and in time was bitten by the bug to enter political life. He left the Navy in 1981, noting that for the first time in the twentieth century a McCain was not serving. His first marriage did not survive the wartime separation, and after a time, McCain met someone new, Cindy Hensley. They married, and McCain moved to Arizona to run for political office. After all, he was someone with a national reputation. The move earned him the sobriquet of "carpetbagger," which clung to him for many years. It is a term he rejects; he married a woman for love, and she just happened to live in Arizona. His first primary for a House seat taught him much, but even after he was elected, he still had something of a chip on his shoulder. In fact, he imagines much later that the *Arizona Republic*, the state's strongest newspaper and one that did not endorse him for president, was "intent on proving that I was intemperate, ungrateful, imperious, selfish, and occasionally corrupt."[18]

One man he praises for showing him the correct path is Herb Drinkwater, a long-term mayor of Scottsdale. After his first election to the House, he came to Scottsdale and was invited to address an out-of-town group of conventioneers. By his own description, his speech was "perfunctory." Then, as McCain tells it, Drinkwater strode to the podium and instantly connected to everyone in the audience by "having a lengthy conversation." Drinkwater "made every single one of them believe that Herb was absolutely delighted to meet them." It was not an act; it was the way Drinkwater governed because he interacted with everyone the same way, even giving people his home phone number. As McCain wrote, "I left the convention with a much broader sense of my job."[19]

McCain proved to be an adept politician and won election to the House. He established his maverick credentials early by coming out against President Ronald Reagan's intervention in Beirut. This took guts because not only was Reagan popular with Republicans in 1983 (if not the country), but he also knew McCain personally and had been friendly and supportive of him. McCain attracted the national media and found himself on television discussing the situation in Lebanon. Tragically, less than a month after McCain spoke in opposition, a suicide bomber blew up a barracks in Beirut, killing 241 Marines, as well as 58 French troops. President Reagan, to his credit, attended the memorial service for the Marines at Camp Lejeune and, as he always did, met with the families of the fallen. With 20 years of hindsight, McCain wrote, "Those responsible for the killing of our Marines escaped without punishment. And to this day we are living with the ramifications of our defeat."[20]

CRISIS IN POLITICS

A few years later, McCain would be burned by an issue nearly wholly of his own making. Charlie Keating, whom to this day McCain describes fondly, was a big-league homebuilder and eventual owner of Lincoln Savings in Arizona; he lived the high life, but he spread the wealth widely to his employees and to people in high office, including McCain, who freely admits enjoying his hospitality in Arizona and the Bahamas. In time, Keating offered more than hospitality; he became a big supporter of McCain and helped to fund his first Senate campaign in 1986.

Shortly after his election, McCain again stood out from his party—the only Republican senator to be named as one of the "Keating Five," a group of senators whom Keating had supported and who were accused of helping him perpetrate his shady dealings. What Keating did at Lincoln Savings, and what others did at other such institutions, caused "the near total destruction of financial institutions that once had been regarded as . . . reliably sound." Resurrecting them cost the federal government the equivalent of $2,000 per person. Ouch!

What McCain had done was what all politicians do for their constituents, but perhaps more aggressively for high-rollers; he listened to their issues and offered advice and influence where legal and appropriate. Eventually, all five senators were called before the Senate Ethics Committee, a humiliating but necessary experience. Of the five, only Alan Cranston was singled out for severe punishment, but that was never pursued. McCain was sent a letter that upheld his innocence but that criticized him for "poor judgment." (Years earlier, McCain also had reimbursed Keating for the cost of flying on his company's corporate jet on vacation trips to the Bahamas.) The experience, which lasted more than four years, shook McCain to the bone. To a degree, he was a victim of partisanship, but he readily admits his own failings. "My reputation for integrity . . . is my responsibility alone, but I learned I cannot protect it if I separate my interests from the public's. I do nothing in secret and keep the whole of my professional life visible to the press."[21]

A RUN ON THE BIG STAGE

Naturally, a political figure such as McCain would gravitate to the national stage and run for the presidency. His 2000 campaign for the Republican nomination was very spirited. To the surprise of many, he won the Michigan primary chiefly because that state's rules allowed voters of any party to select a primary candidate. It was a blow to George W. Bush's campaign and on the heels of a heated exchange McCain had with Bush on CNN's *Larry King Live* during a candidate's debate-style panel discussion. Political operatives in South Carolina had planted scurrilous lies and innuendos playing up racial hatred and inferring that McCain was the father of a black child and therefore was unfit to lead. (He and wife Cindy have adopted a daughter from Bangladesh.) McCain assumed that Bush was behind it, though he denied it. The exchange revealed McCain's temper, well known but not advertised; it also demonstrated that McCain is a man of principle.

However, McCain faulted himself in that same South Carolina campaign. When asked about the Confederate flag flying atop the state capitol, he said such a choice was up to the people of the state, not the federal government. He calls that statement "a moment of cowardice." Imagine a politician admitting such a thing, let alone one who had faced far graver terrors as a POW. McCain sought to right his wrong and later journeyed back to South Carolina and apologized. As he writes reflectively in *Why Courage Matters*, "The lesson that I took from that experience was this: In the long run, you're far better off taking the courageous path."[22]

Bush, of course, went on to win the 2000 election, and in 2004, McCain actively supported him to the consternation of many voters, either Democrat or Independent, who liked McCain's stand on the issues. "How could he?" was a common complaint. In that election, McCain was doing what all successful politicians do—standing up for their base. As a Republican, McCain likely felt a duty to support a Republican for president, even one running against a friendly Senate colleague, John Kerry. McCain does not hesitate to speak his mind. When criticized by Speaker of the House Dennis Hastert for protesting the tax cuts in a time of war, McCain positioned himself above the fray. "I yearn for the days when the Republican Party was the party of fiscal discipline and conservatism." While extending an olive branch to party leadership, McCain insisted, "[T]here's nothing that we do in Washington that compares to the service and sacrifice of these young men and women. I just don't want them to come back to a bankrupt country." Their commitment, McCain believes, out-weighs partisanship.[23]

HAND ACROSS THE AISLE

McCain is better known for working both sides of the aisle. In 2005, he teamed with Senator Ted Kennedy, the icon of the liberal left, to develop a new policy on immigration. As the senator of a state that borders Mexico, the issue is critical to his constituents. The new law would be tough on lawbreakers who seek to exploit the illegals but demonstrates mercy and compassion for those coming to this nation for a better life. McCain is conservative by nature and voting record, but for him, comity in legislature is something he values. For example, he decided not to support fellow Republican, Senate Majority Leader Bill Frist on the so-called nuclear option that would eliminate a senator's right to filibuster. "Look, we won't always be the majority," he reminded his Republican colleagues. "Second of all, we ought to be able to work it out. Third of all, I don't want to shut down the Senate. We're in a war. . . . Shouldn't we be doing the people's busi-ness?"[24] In May 2005, McCain's logic prevailed. He helped to broker a compromise with fellow senators from both sides of the political aisle to guarantee the right of filibuster, as well as the promise to allow full Senate votes on certain judicial nomi-nees. This was a temporary solution perhaps, but another example of McCain's influence.

McCain's greatest bit of bipartisanship occurred with the pas-sage of the McCain-Feingold Act to reform campaign funding. The act outlaws so-called soft spending for or against candidates by political action committees (PACs). The law also stipulates that every political ad carry the imprimatur of the candidate, as in "I'm Senator So-and-so, and I support this ad." Such identi-fication, it was hoped, would prevent candidates from hiding behind smokescreens in disclaiming attack ads. Loopholes, of course, were found in campaign funding, but McCain-Feingold was a bold step in the right direction. And it was born out of McCain's own missteps with campaign funding in the "Keating Five" affair nearly 20 years earlier.

McCain's ire was raised by the Abu Gharib affair, the prisoner abuse scandal that blew the lid off the mistreatment of Iraqi prisoners. As a former POW, he had no sympathy for the perpetrators. As he told CNN's Larry King, "We've always prided ourselves, Americans have, on treating prisoners according to the Geneva Convention." McCain added that German POWs interned in Arizona during the World War II held "reunions." To the argument that the prisoners were not soldiers, McCain acknowledged the difference between Al Qaeda and ordinary Iraqi prisoners but cautioned that not all U.S. troops in Iraq are always in "in uniform." Most clearly, and with the voice of experience, McCain emphasized his central argument: "[W]hy do we respect the Geneva Conventions? . . . [B]ecause we want our men and women, if held captive, to be treated in a decent and human fashion."[25]

McCain is one of those rare men in government who can combine a love of sport and actual work. McCain chaired a Senate investigation into steroid use in baseball in 2004, a full year before a special committee of the House did the same. McCain was less concerned with professional athletes and more concerned with younger athletes. "The real problem," he told ABC's *Good Morning America,* "is the high school athletes who believe the only way they're going to make it in professional baseball is to use these performance-enhancing drugs." McCain went on to delineate the down side, "Whether it be liver disease or heart attack, stroke or psychological problems, [such drugs] can be devastating to young people."[26] Sadly, one year later, before a House committee investigating the same issue, parents of high school athletes who had died from steroid abuse supported what McCain, along with many health professionals, had been reporting. It was at the House hearing that famous baseball players testified, after which McCain said that baseball "[C]an't be trusted." McCain "applauded . . . colleagues in the House because what this [hearing] highlighted was the absolute insensitivity of both the owners and the players to the American people." McCain also said, "[W]e ought to consider . . . a law that says all professional sports have a minimum level of performance-enhancing drug testing." He also revealed his love for baseball in expressing disappointment in former home run slugger Mark McGwire's refusal at the House hearings to confront his or other players' alleged use of steroids. "I was saddened by what he had to say, and it's unfortunate because he's one of America's heroes."[27]

ON REFLECTION

McCain is an accomplished author. With writer Mark Salter, an aide, he has produced three best-selling tomes. *Faith of Our Fathers* details his upbringing in a family steeped in naval tradition, as well as his own high-spirited life as a naval cadet, Navy pilot, and most powerfully, his searing experiences as a POW. *Worth Fighting For* details the experiences that shaped his political life, as well as affectionate insights into politicians such as President Ronald Reagan, Congressman Morris Udall, and Senators Barry Goldwater and John Tower. *Why Courage Matters* is an eloquent tribute to the power of courage and its importance in both public and private life. It reminds one of another senator's work from a generation before, *Profiles in Courage,* by John F. Kennedy. Taken together, the books provide a sketch of McCain's world view that is intimate in detail about the forces and circumstances that shaped him, revelatory about his personal failings, and triumphant in his commitment to values that he believes will make America not simply a military power to be reckoned with but a force for positive influence.

McCain's writing reveals something else. Russell Baker, former columnist for the *New York Times*, wrote in the *New York Review of Books* that *Worth Fighting For* "is the work of someone who has found out . . . who he is and what he truly believes. Self-discovery seems to give [McCain] the nerve to speak his mind with a candor rare among politicians."[28] Reflection is a powerful communication tool because it provides insight into a leader's core strength: his sense of self. He cops to a strong temper that has gotten him into hot water on multiple occasions; for example during his first election, he struck back at a questioner who accused him of "apparent opportunism" by confessing that he had moved around his whole life, saying sarcastically, "[T]he place I lived the longest in my life was Hanoi." McCain also admits that his "wise ass" sense of humor can appear mean-spirited. During his first run for the Senate, he spoke of the civic mindedness of Arizona's elderly, jocularly referring to some as living in "Seizure World." He later castigates himself and then defends himself by promoting his support for issues affecting the elderly without saying what he should have said—"I'm sorry."[29] Both incidents occurred early in his political career, and he has put both to bed many times over. McCain has grown up; he knows how life in the public arena can twist words into swords intentionally or not. And he has resolved to do better.

Where John McCain goes from here will be a matter of destiny and history. But his legacy will be one of a man sometimes pugnacious, always valorous, who gave back to his country more than it gave to him. He invested his popularity wisely, enabling him to pass reform legislation on political fundraising, as well as other initiatives. Of course, he will be forever defined by the years he spent in captivity as a POW, a period that weakened him physically but toughened him emotionally and spiritually and sent him on a path of service for which many are grateful.

Leadership Lessons

- *Learn from your mistakes.* Through every phase of his life, John McCain has demonstrated what it means to do the right thing. He has made mistakes in his life, some public and some private. He has learned from them and resolved to make a positive difference.

- *Reach across the aisle.* In an era of bitter political polarization, John McCain has the strength of conviction to seek allies for his cause in both parties. Neither a party hardliner nor a go-with-the-flow person, McCain seeks consensus as a means of good government.

- *Make courage tangible.* Many people have a perception that you have to be larger than life to show courage. John McCain dispels that notion in his life, as well as in his writings; he demonstrates that courage is a resolution to face the odds, even when it is dangerous, in order to do something positive for your friend, your family, or your country.

- *Look to the future.* After spending so much time in captivity and recuperation, John McCain could have ended up a bitter man. Instead, he has channeled his energy into personal healing, as well as reaching out to people on all sides of issues. He even returned to Vietnam with fellow Vietnam veteran Senator John Kerry to investigate reports of troops missing in action.

- *Speak up for what you believe.* Taking a stand is essential to leadership. McCain voices his opinions on a diverse set of issues and then resolves to take action, be it political, social, or personal.

- *Live your values.* John McCain was raised in a culture that valued national service. As a naval aviator and U.S. senator, McCain has served his country with distinction and in the process served as an example to his fellow troops, senators, and citizens.

Transpire

- *Results—when goals are fulfilled*

*R*esults come from the fulfillment of vision achieved through execution and discipline, as well as a willingness to explore alternatives along the way that may involve risk but always courage. What transpires are intended results, ones that will endure because they are sustained by the commitment of leaders and followers together.

C H A P T E R

"Our real competitor is, in many ways, the old way of doing things."[1]

Meg Whitman
CEO, eBay

RESULTS

TWO KINDS OF RESULTS

Playing sports as a youth is a character-building experience. Young people learn the value of discipline, preparation, and training, as well as resilience, teamwork, and results. No sport better exemplifies such preparation than football. Military generals from MacArthur to Eisenhower have extolled the game. Legendary coach Vince Lombardi used to show General MacArthur Army game films when he (Lombardi) was an assistant football coach at the United States Military Academy. For these men, football was preparation for life.

Bob Ladouceur at De La Salle High School would not disagree, but after coaching for 26 years, he also realizes that football is a sport and a part of life, not the other way around. To some coaches, this would be heresy. Not to Ladouceur. And he has the stats to back up his holistic point of view. From 1992 through 2003, his football team did not lose a single game; it won 12 consecutive Division 1A state titles and was given a number one ranking in USA Today, the team's fourth such consecutive ranking and fifth in six years.[2] While some coaches preach a kind of athletic apartheid—athletes keeping to themselves to build discipline and cohesion—football at De La Salle complements life. Athletes integrate themselves with the school and the community.

Football at the school begins with Ladouceur. While he has been coaching for three decades, he did not begin his adult life as a coach; he was probation officer. That was good preparation for taking over a losing football program at a school with a small student body and consequently an undermanned football team. Ladouceur was all of 25 years old when he was hired to coach and teach religious studies, a dual load he carries to this day.

"My approach is all about process," says Ladouceur, reflecting on how he taught the team to play and himself to coach. "I just said to myself, 'Let's teach these guys how to win and what it takes to win, and they make it a day-to-day process.'" After instruction, players are expected to teach themselves, as well as others, on and off the field. Like all good teachers, though, Ladouceur uses mistakes as a learning tool. "It's all about teachable moments and being aware of teachable moments when they occur." As Ladouceur says, "The fortunate thing about having 50 kids, there's a teachable moment every day."[3]

As much as Ladouceur may remind others of other winning coaches, he is his own man. "I never tried to pattern myself after a coach or any one person. You have to be yourself. If you're not who you say you are, the people you are with, in my case the kids, will find out quickly."[4] This is important at De La Salle, which has a small student body of 1,000 students. Such size has dictated that Ladouceur maximize his resources; he does this by keeping things simple. His offense runs off two plays—the option and the "veer"—both of which require a heady quarterback and synchronicity of all players pulling together as one. As Dan Wallace, author of a book on De La Salle writes, size is less important than teamwork based on trust and execution.[5]

Off-season training begins in January, a month after the end of the championships in December. But team bonding does not stay in the weight room; it continues throughout a myriad of outdoor activities, such as camping and rafting, as well as volunteer work and chapel. As Ladouceur says, "If a team has no soul, you're just wasting your time."[6]

The tight-knit De La Salle community was rocked in the summer of 2004 when Terrance Kelly, most valuable player of the 2003 unbeaten team and headed for the University of Oregon on a football scholarship, was killed in a shooting. Some 1,500 people turned out for his funeral. It was a tribute to the young man, as well as to what De La Salle means to the community—and, in turn, to what football meant to the fallen player. At the start of the 2004 season with the team's emotions raw, Kelly's family sought to rally the team. According to Terry Edison, the school's athletic director and team's defensive coordinator, the family was "telling them that [Kelly] would want them to play hard."[7]

Results at De La Salle are not measured on the scoreboard or in the rankings. Just prior to the start of 2004, when the streak had reached 151 games, Ladouceur said, "I'm sure that there's built-in pressure. But that doesn't come from our program. . . . The kids know what's important to us, [and] maintaining the streak is not the most important thing at all. I want to see them maximize their ability . . . play with heart and character and soul."[8] On September 4, 2004, the streak ended, and as is typical of everything at De La Salle, the team handled it in a dignified manner; after the game, De La Salle players shook hands with the other team. Ladouceur congratulated the winners by saying, "I'm all for everybody playing good football and getting better. If our level of play helped Bellevue [Washington] prepare and raise their play, that's great. I think there should be lots of kinds of the mountain, not just one."[9]

Lasting success is measured in the hearts and minds of the generations of young men who have played football for Ladouceur and emerged the better for it. They have matriculated to college, found good jobs, married, and most important to Ladouceur, found ways to make their own contributions to family, work, and community.

⚬◈ ◈⚬

Normally an appearance on CBS's 60 Minutes *would be a company's worse nightmare, the information age's equivalent of being in the stockade of public opinion. Not so for SAS, a privately held computer company located in Cary, North Carolina. Correspondent Morley Safer, not noted for being soft on anyone except entertainers, positively exuded accolades for SAS as he toured the facilities, interviewed employees, and sat down with the founder and chairman, Jim Goodnight.*

Not surprisingly, people do not leave SAS. Despite periodic implosions within the information technology (IT) business, SAS is remarkably stable; the company hires while others fire. Its human resources policies seem to be have been written by utopian social scientists rather than by business professionals. Aside from the onsite day care, fitness centers, and subsidized cafeterias that many enlightened companies offer, SAS provides onsite medical care for employees and dependents, as well as concierge-style services for life questions related to children's schooling, elder care, and financial planning.

There is a business side; the more cares the company can remove from employees, the more the employees can focus on their work and careers. SAS seeks to create a virtuous cycle of benefits-enrichment-productivity. Another way that SAS retains its employees is through what Goodnight calls, "freedom of move-

ment." SAS provides opportunities for people to change jobs. "If you get tired of your old job, you do something new." This mantra has enabled SAS to provide challenges to employees and in the process provide them with opportunities to grow their skills and continue to contribute to the enterprise.[10]

Not surprisingly, SAS is a culture of stories. The company's Web site features "Success Stories," tales of what SAS has accomplished for its customers, as well as what employees have contributed. Some stories include video features on client successes using SAS software solutions. Furthermore, the company's in-house journal, sas.com magazine, *combines management advice as well as insights into IT trends. SAS is a culture rich in communications: employees to employees, company to customer, and leaders to leaders.*

SAS is not a nonprofit or a philanthropist; it is a closely held business with an array of impressive software products. It claims to be the "leader in business intelligence and analytics, giving you the complete vision to learn from the past, monitor and communicate the present, and gain insight into the future." This is not a bad statement for what leaders need to do. Final proof of results is in the numbers. According to a corporate press release, SAS posted revenues of $1.53 billion in 2004, continuing its "unbroken track record of revenue growth and profitability." It has every indication of continuing. SAS leads its industry in "percentage of revenue invested in research and development at 25 percent." Results beget results![11]

ꙮ ꙮ

A faster chip. Increasing sales. Reduced absenteeism. A Food and Drug Administration (FDA)–approved drug. More access. Rising stock valuations. Improved quality. Improved customer service. Peace. You can sum all these achievements with a single word—*results!* For Bob Ladouceur at De La Salle, results were measured not simply by victories on the field but also by victories in the classroom and in the hearts and minds of the young men who played for him. For Bob Goodnight, results are measured on the bottom line but developed by people whom SAS nurtures with exceptional attentiveness. Leadership is all about achieving results, making things—products, services, and people—*better*.

Results are what happen when vision, alignment, execution, and discipline flow together, not necessarily seamlessly, but all in the same direction. Achieving results is what every leader, and indeed every follower, in an organization wants. Why else do you work other than to achieve something? To ensure that you really achieve what you want to achieve, it is always good to go back to two questions: why and how? "Why" flows from your vision and mission; "how" begins with alignment. Organizations typically are well focused on vision; they know where they want to go. It is in the getting there that things get tough. For this reason, in this chapter about results, it is worthwhile to reframe alignment in the context of results.

UNITY OF PURPOSE

Alignment is the unity of purpose that brings people together for a similar cause. In business, however, alignment runs deeper. You can define it as coming together behind specific strategies, objectives, and even tactics. Alignment is a form of agreement that unites people and enables them to work together. Communication is the key driver of alignment, but so often it is overlooked. Executives at the top feel that if they state the objective once, it will be carried out—as if by magic. Would that this were true! One former CEO at a major manufacturer used to speak in frustration about initiatives being bogged down within a "layer of clay," which he defined as middle management. This CEO was not maligning his people but rather lamenting the bureaucracy that would absorb an initiative and bury it, often because it would not seem important by the time it reached its intended audiences. This was a failure of alignment.

It is not enough simply to communicate, nor even to listen. You must communicate and listen *with purpose*. There is a remarkable communication model for achieving organizational alignment, and it was developed by a client of mine, Gene Schutt, a senior executive in the financial services industry. Throughout his 30-year career, Gene has either participated in or led a number of change initiatives. Experience has taught him the value of communication but, more important, communication for alignment, which he calls the "aligned action model." While Gene would be the last person to take credit for it, and while it does draw on other communication models, I think Gene's model is worthy of exploration for two reasons: First, it's easy to follow, and, second, it works. There are four steps in the aligned action model, and I will take them one at a time.[12]

- *Information.* Alignment begins with information—providing people with the data they will need to make informed decisions about the initiative. Such information should relate to the vision and mission of the organization, as well as to the specific strategies. Steve Jobs, CEO of Apple, is a master at relating information that will move people to action. When he delivers a keynote address at an Apple product launch, he generates excitement about the new product by placing it into the context of Apple's product line, as well as Apple's vision for technology and consumer lifestyles. With Jobs, there is always a bit of inspiration to go along with the information, which makes for a powerful message.

- *Understanding.* Once people have information, they form a mental picture of what must be done. All too often, senior-level managers stop communicating about the initiative, thinking that they have done their jobs. Far from it! Now they must go out and sell it to their people to promote understanding. Part of the sales process involves listening. Leaders must ask people for feedback, capturing and incorporating their thoughts and suggestions. Most specifically, leaders must ensure that people know what their jobs are and what they must do to fulfill the strategy. A good example of understanding emerges from observation of volunteer social service groups. People in such organizations, which may do everything from providing clothing and shelter to seeking an eradication of land mines, understand the mission of their organization. Furthermore, they understand their role in that organization, be it to build a house, collect food, or raise funds. Their leadership continually reminds them of the mission, and people subscribe to it.

Schutt cautions managers not to underestimate the time it takes to generate genuine understanding. Too many managers want to jump the gun and move ahead without waiting for people to process new information. Critical to the understanding process, says Schutt, is providing reasons why a change is necessary. "Not to share reasons why makes people wonder why," Schutt explains. Understanding may occur anywhere from within a matter of hours to within a matter of months; patience and continued communication are essential.

FUZZY ZONE

Now we enter the fuzzy zone. Information leads naturally to understanding, but moving to the next step—commitment—requires a leap of faith. It is up to the leaders to demonstrate good faith, that is, that what they are telling people about and what people have come to understand are in the best interest of the organization. Every single change initiative faces this dilemma. People may understand intellectually, but unless they can feel that the change is good for them, there will be resistance and subsequently a lack of commitment. And this is where leadership enters the picture.

- *Commitment.* When issues are well communicated and backed by sincerity and example, they can move forward to the next step—commitment. When people know their roles and believe in them, as well as in their leaders, they are far more likely to make a commitment—but only when they trust that their leader has their best interests at heart. Toward this end, leaders must be front and center, communicating by listening and learning from what people are saying or perhaps not saying. A leader who is attuned to what is happening in her organization has a better opportunity to push for change. As discussed earlier, Toyota has reduced its quest for increased market share to two words: Global 15. This slogan refers to the company's desire to gain 15 percent of the world's automotive market.[13] What is important to realize is that employees at every level in Toyota know what they must do to deliver on it; strategies and objectives have been aligned with its fulfillment. In this way, a simple slogan becomes a pathway to success.

- *Aligned action.* Knowing what to do is the not the same as doing it. Execution is the follow-through step in the aligned action model. Once more, leaders must push for execution, getting people to follow through. A prime example of action in alignment with organizational goals is the performance of the New England Patriots in 2004. Coach Bill Belichick is a master at communicating the big picture, as well as breaking game plans down into executable points. Moreover, together with his players, he has fostered a culture where players will do whatever it takes to win. For example, in 2004, Troy Brown, a veteran receiver, moved to defensive back when injuries sidelined Ty Law. Linebacker Mike Vrabel sometimes played running back. Within the Patriots, there is an expectation of excellence, and everyone does his part to fulfill it. Coaches and players are informed, understand their roles, are committed to their goals, and act in alignment to win. As a result, the Patriots won the Super Bowl three times in four years.

ACHIEVING RESULTS

When explaining the aligned action model, Schutt uses a sailing regatta as a metaphor. As Schutt explains, "If you think about the crews, [you know that] they've studied the race plan. They understand what they have to do, and they are committed to winning. Everyone is sailing in the same direction." It is an example of aligned action in motion, and it is especially apt for organizations with facilities in multiple locations. Each business unit is like a sailboat; it's up to the captain of each boat to use the wind to his advantage to round the race buoys and reach the finish ahead of the competition.

The net result of informing, understanding, committing, and acting in alignment is the fulfillment of strategies and objectives. In other words, you deliver results pure and simple. Ideally, by seeking understanding and commitment, people will be working cooperatively so that actions flow smoothly. This, of course, is not reality. Product development projects are fraught with peril, and despite best intentions, they may suffer multiple setbacks until the product is ready for market. In fact, the model itself can be used when facing roadblocks; getting people together for information, understanding, commitment, and action will enable people to tackle the problem and move forward. Alignment is preserved, and actions go forward.

STRIVING FOR LASTING RESULTS

Following the aligned action model in sequence is essential. It is tempting to skip from inform to act; it happens most of the time in organizations. And it may be why so many change initiatives fail. On the other hand, you really cannot develop understanding or commitment if people do not know the issues and the context. Action is the logical outflow of these four steps, so you increase your chances of success when you follow them in order.

Following the steps of the model is one thing; doing it with purpose is another. The success of this communication model is not the process; it's the outcome, that is, what you accomplish. Accomplishment can occur only when managers take the time not simply to listen but also to learn from their people. Understanding is enriched by the interaction that occurs between manager and employee. The employee begins to learn what is expected, and the manager learns what she can expect in terms of performance. This understanding phase typically does not occur overnight but rather over a period of weeks and months.

The purpose of leadership is, of course, results. However, lasting results will occur only when people know their jobs and trust one another. They become committed to organizational goals and, in turn, want to deliver on the strategies and objectives. Alignment is critical to results, and it can occur only if managers are willing to invest themselves in the communication process to bring people together for common cause, the aligned actions for success.

OVERCOMING RESISTANCE

A manager using the aligned action model would do well to keep another model in mind; it is the *change model formula*. Expressed as $D \times V \times F > R$, this equation underscores the fact that the success of a change initiative must compound the forces of dissatisfaction (D) with the status quo, vision of the future (V), and the need to take action, that is, first steps (F), to overcome resistance to change (R).[14]

Managers who overlook what is happening now and do not communicate the benefits of doing things differently to achieve a new vision will not be able to implement anything new and different, be it a new process, a new accounting system, or a wholesale organizational transformation. However, developing a stream of communications that acknowledges employee dissatisfaction, promotes the power of the vision, and describes first steps will overcome inertia and resistance and enable the manager to push for real change. In reality, the $D \times V \times F > R$ formula can be incorporated into communications related to the information, understanding, and commitment stages.

TURNING RESULTS INTO NEWS

Results, therefore, are to be celebrated, cherished, and remembered. They are the fodder for stories. Communicating results is important. Public companies report results quarterly and issue annual reports. Nonprofits publish annual statements. In fact, just about every organization of any kind takes a moment to write up what it has been doing and tell the world about it. This is good as far as it goes, but it's only a starting point.

Pfizer, for example, includes stories of people who have helped produce their drugs, as well as stories of patients who have been helped by them. Ford Motor Company issues an annual corporate citizen report that includes stories about what the company has done to improve society in terms of technology and the environment. Other organizations from universities to public school systems, as well as hospitals and social service agencies, tell similar tales. What these stories do is give the result the human touch. Human beings, to paraphrase an adage, do not live by numbers alone. We seek meaning. Stories add depth and context to what has occurred.

Even numbers have a role to play, however. Sales organizations live by results—incremental increases to volume, revenue, and profit. These numbers are important and are published within the organization and disseminated widely. Manufacturers, too, live by numbers—reductions in defects, improvements to processes, and increases in speed are tangible successes that mark progress. It is up to the leadership to proclaim the numbers and talk about the faces behind the numbers. Annual sales conventions laud the good numbers and tell stories about the individual achievers. Many plants have print or Web newsletters that do the same. Such public measures are important.

DRIVING RESULTS

Achieving results emerges from the vision, alignment, and discipline required. When the results are posted, it is time to tell stories. Leaders need to be front and center on this effort.

- *Mark milestones.* Once upon a time, drivers through rural America were amused by signs for Burma Shave; the sayings were corny, but they helped pass the time. Burma Shave billboards marked the journey. Plan in advance what the milestones of your journey from vision through fulfillment will be. Create stories about what things will be like as you reach each milestone. For example, during a product development cycle, the unveiling of the prototype can be an occasion for a get-together. Automotive companies have been known to unveil prototypes at auto shows. You may not wish to get that elaborate, but make certain that prototypes are seen and heard around the organization. Stories arise from these kinds of accomplishments.

- *Celebrate achievements.* Take time out to celebrate an achievement. It may be a prototype, or it may be the acknowledgment of improved quality or enhanced software solutions. Achievements become stories suitable for an internal newsletter or even a trade publication. Post such achievements on the Web site. You want everyone to know that you are making progress.

- *Recognize the contributors.* So often people work not simply for money but also for recognition. The recognition can be as elaborate as an award and resort vacation for two in the Bahamas or as simple as a pat on the back. Invite the contributors to tell their stories, and post those stories on the Web site. (*Hint:* Recognize people the way they want to be recognized. Some of us are shy and prefer to stay out of the limelight; if so, respect that person's privacy.)

- *Demonstrate engagement.* Leaders need to be visible when results are posted. It is traditional for the CEO and board of directors to be present at annual shareholder meetings. This is one form of story. But it must be repeated in different forms and in different ways throughout the year and throughout the organization. For years, the Kellogg Company has held a "State of the Company" meeting for all employees; the CEO and key executives address employees about the state of the business. It's simple and straightforward, but it demonstrates that the senior leaders care enough about their people to keep them informed and also that they value results and want to keep them coming.

The theme of the preceding is spreading the glory, allowing everyone his or her moment to shine. And this is important to remember when noting results: It is not processes or applications that ultimately generate results. It is people and their applied wisdom that make things happen. Noting the occasion reminds everyone of the humanity of the enterprise and keeps energy levels high going forward.

INTENDED VERSUS UNINTENDED RESULTS

On the quest for results, it is useful to keep in mind that all results are not intended, nor are all unintended results bad. For example, Viagra is the unintended result of a medicine to control blood pressure. It was not successful in that application, but it achieved considerable success elsewhere in men's bodies. Likewise, the development of ink jet printers came about when an engineer discovered by accident how to apply ink in novel ways. These are serendipitous events.

However, most often unintended results are unwelcome. And they occur with greater frequency as organizations go faster and faster. Sometimes the unintended result is a failed product launch or a miserable service offering or poorly conceived software application. Many of these failures could have been corrected with a better vision, stricter alignment, sharper execution, or better discipline. However, as in the case of a drug failure in human trials, all progressed nicely. To fail is human. The U.S. Marines make a habit of celebrating failure not out of a sense of misanthropy or desire to punish the perpetrator but because the Marines realize that by studying what went wrong, they can prevent similar mistakes in the future.[15]

Unintended results are not always failures per se; they are incomplete or not fully satisfied results. If you want to increase sales by 50 percent and you achieve 40 percent growth, this is still pretty good. It's a "failure" of 10 percent, but it may have been caused by a product glitch, a collapse of a customer, a tight economy, or any number of factors outside the parameter of the sales force. Likewise, if an organization is unable to achieve a quality metric but improves the product, this is a mark of achievement.

Unintended results regarding people, such as work overload, high absenteeism, burnout, or leaving the company, are not causes for celebration. These may mean that the vision was too lofty and the bar too high, or that execution and discipline were too strict, and while the results may have been achieved, the human toll may have been unacceptable. Combat is a good example of this paradigm; casualties are expected in conflict but never, ever accepted. (It must be said that when underachieving people leave an organization, it is not necessarily an occasion for mourning. It may be a harbinger of better results to come, because those who stay are those who are committed. As the sign in the Michigan football team's locker-room says, "Those who stay will be champions.")

It is a mistake to try to hide unintended results. They are stories, too. An inability to acknowledge a shortcoming is a shortcoming of leadership, not necessarily a shortcoming of employees. Speak up and resolve to do better. People respect leaders who demonstrate a sense of vulnerability.

A MATTER OF CONFIDENCE

Now, when you achieve the intended result, the natural outcome is immense satisfaction. This emotion leads to a stronger belief in yourself and your organization. What we call *confidence!* Using this word as the title of her new book, Harvard professor Rosabeth Moss Kanter writes, "Confidence is the bridge connecting expectations and performance, investments and results." Winning organizations have it in spades; losing teams cannot seem to spell it. Yet, as Kanter points out, confidence is necessary for success.[16] Why? Because confidence is that inner fire that says that we can do it if we try. It also is that inner voice that knows when to ask for help. For example, Michael Jordan did not win a championship without a smart coach and a savvy supporting team. Fred Smith did not build the world's most successful air freight system without a superior team of logisticians and dedicated pilots. Confidence is knowledge of one's own strengths as well as of one's own limitations. In other words, you need to know when to say you can go it alone and when to call in reinforcements. As such, confidence is a valuable leadership trait. Here are some ways to nurture it:[17]

- *Invite your workers to look up.* Leadership, by nature, is inspirational. It must make people want to achieve. Leaders play their part by setting goals and inviting others to add to those goals. For example, a sales manager may set a goal of achieving $1 million in new sales per month. A turned-on sales team will take this as a challenge and strive to bring in an additional $100,000 in new monthly business. When they do, team members feel good about themselves and want to keep on achieving. In sales, we call this the *swagger.* A sales team without swagger is like a ship without a rudder, drifting on a sea of apathy.

- *Let your workers see you sweat.* Yes, this is the reverse of the Broadway adage. However, I am not talking acting; I'm talking real life. Confidence comes from working the details, from being willing to become part of the team and sharing the load with them. It is honed by discipline and attentiveness. This is not micromanagement; it's a sharing of burdens. And when things turn around and goals are met, it's a sharing of glory earned by the sweat of the collective brow.

- *Learn from your mistakes.* John Madden, America's leading football analyst, has said, "Coaches have to watch for what they don't want to see and listen for what they don't want to hear." What Madden means is that it is human nature to avoid confronting mistakes, especially if the mistakes are being committed by people for whom you are responsible. This is folly. Mistakes are learning opportunities. Capitalize on them as learning lessons. When you correct them properly, you likely will not repeat them. And that has to inspire a degree of confidence.

- *Radiate hope.* Nelson Mandela spent 27 years in prison for the cause of African nationalism in South Africa. Throughout those long years of deprivation without family, he did not lose hope in the righteousness of his cause. Dr. Kanter cites Mandela as a model of confidence. Mandela embodied the hope of his nation, first to his followers inside prison and then to those outside. He showed just how hopeful he was when he became president of the new South Africa. He did not seek retribution; he sought reconciliation, which, in the long run, was the only way to avoid bloodshed and integrate economic, political, and global resources. And by doing so, he provided hope for all the people of South Africa.[18]

A KEY DIFFERENCE MAKER

Of course, you can be too confident. For example, after the devastation of World War I, the French built the Maginot Line, a fortified wall of concrete and armaments designed to keep the Germans from ever attacking again. The French government put its faith in the wall; the Nazis ignored the wall and entered France through the Low Countries. The Nazis, too, had their own line of defense, the Siegfried Line, which, of course, the Allies blew threw via air, artillery, and tank power. Overconfidence prevents companies from seeing the dangers lurking over the corporate parking lot; these may include anything from a changing market to a new competitor or a breakthrough product.

Nonetheless, confidence is essential to leadership. A leader without confidence can neither guide nor inspire; such a leader can only sit in the shadows while others carry the load. Confidence is a unifier that brings people together because it feeds on their collective energies. Confident organizations are those that succeed because they draw on the strengths of their leaders and followers pulling together for a common cause. A genuinely confident leader is one who knows herself, her people, and her abilities to move an organization forward to achieve its goals.

VALUE EQUATION

The lasting measure of results is the value. Did the result add value to the organization? So often in business, results are important only to the organization, not to the customer. For example, a company takes pride when it reduces costs, waste, and absenteeism. All these things are friction on the system; they detract from the enterprise. While important, however, they do not add value directly to the customer. Customers care about price, service, and benefits; they do not care what a company does inside. Customers want to do business with companies that are efficient not because they are cost-cutters but because they deliver those savings to the customer in terms of improved performance.

All too often companies laud themselves too loudly for cutting costs when what they should be doing instead is finding ways to add value. Cutting costs is an accounting exercise; it is important, yes, but straightforward. Adding value is the art of business. How you add value means what you put into the offering to make the lives of customers better. The benefits may be a more fuel-efficient vehicle, a faster response time on loan approvals, more attentive service from health care providers, or direct access to help lines that offer personal assistance. These things make a difference in customers' lives; they are measures of value that mean something to people.

Such measures of value have an internal component, too. Employees want to know that what they do is adding value to someone's life. They also want to be valued for their contributions. Results that matter to customers will matter to employees, too. Stories of how customers made use of product improvements or enjoyed an improved service option will reinforce the value of what employees do. When employees learn that their work makes people's lives better, it makes them feel connected to their end users and a contributor to their welfare and well-being.

SUSTAINING RESULTS

Results emerge from a well-conceived vision, a fully aligned team and organization, savvy execution, and rigorous discipline. Meg Whitman sees value emerging from the collective efforts of the users as well as the legions of satisfied customers. She promotes this value story inside and outside eBay and in this way helps to drive the company forward. The challenges met and overcome are to be recognized, in particular because the nature of organizations calls for continuous results. Sustaining success is called for. The process for repeating results is the same as achieving them. Sometimes visions can remain constant; other times they must shift with the times. For example, a successful pharmaceutical company may shift to gene therapy. This calls for a new kind of alignment, new forms of execution, and continuously applied discipline. Sports teams, in contrast, rise and fall annually according to games won. A vision may remain the same, but with new players, changes occur that necessitate new alliances. Execution of fundamentals and discipline in accordance with physical and mental standards increases.

The fact that you need to repeat your success should not detract from the moment. In fact, it should inspire the next accomplishment. Organizational life is not about resting on laurels; it is about looking for the next hill to climb, the next challenge to meet, the next goal to achieve. Legend says that Alexander the Great fell to his knees and cried when he discovered that there were no more lands to be conquered. Reality was more that his generals convinced him that enough was enough; Alexander's armies had already conquered all of Persia and had moved into the Indian subcontinent. The soldiers were homesick.[19] Alexander was a wise enough leader to let them return. After the victory at the Battle of Hydaspes, Alexander's armies had achieved all that they could achieve, and it was time to celebrate and enjoy the fruits of victory. Today's leaders in both the public and private sectors would do well to remember Alexander's example. (*Note:* Alexander himself was no pushover; he was one of history's bloodiest generals, but even he knew when enough was enough.[20])

Results also lay the groundwork for who comes next. Those who led once may decide to hand the reins to those who played supporting roles. In this way, the vision, alignment, execution, and discipline processes renew themselves with new blood, new ideas, and new commitments. This is the way of successful organizations. And it is a form of achievement in itself. It is a result that, while not final, continues to produce.

Results Story Planner

Achieving results is an accomplishment. Consider the following questions to help you think of ways to demonstrate that results matter. Think of stories to support the results.

- How will you mark milestones in your organization?
- How will you celebrate what you have achieved?
- How will you demonstrate that you are engaged and that other people need to be engaged in the process?

- How will you sustain the results? What will you need to do to get people to understand the need to keep focused on the vision?

Communication Action Steps (Results)

- *Aspire.* How we push ourselves to succeed.
- *Perspire.* What we did to put ourselves into a position to succeed.
- *Require.* What we did to execute results.
- *Transpire.* How we pushed ourselves to succeed.

MEG WHITMAN

It has been said many times that leadership is fired in the cauldrons of crisis. If this is true, then Meg Whitman faced her own test of leadership in an e-cauldron in June 1999 when the eBay site crashed. Web sites crash with regularity, and even eBay's went down occasionally, but this time it was different. The site, on which thousands of people depend for their livelihood, millions patronize for merchandise, and billions are earned in commissions, would not come back up. "I did the only thing I knew what to do—be there!" said Whitman five years later. So what could a CEO with no computer training possibly do in this technological meltdown? Two things. First, her presence would send a signal to eBay's tech providers that the crisis was serious and that she expected to get their best attention. "I could call Scott McNealy at Sun, . . . Ray Lane at Oracle, or Mark Leslie at Veritas and say, 'I need you.'" Second, it provided a measure of support for her tech team, who camped out for the duration.[21]

After three days, the site returned, but not functionally. Pierre Omidyar, the computer programmer who founded eBay, entered the fray. Whitman asked, "What if they can't fix it?" As Whitman recalls, Omidyar replied, "Usually when it gets this bad, it means they're just a few hours from figuring it out." Omidyar was right; hours later an Oracle technician figured out the solution, and the site was up and running. The drama was not over for Whitman; she took it on herself to make certain that it would never happen again. She plunged herself into technology issues to get up to speed. "It was total immersion." One problem was "leadership of the technology team," recalls Omidyar; changes were made. One executive says, "She's [Whitman's] the most down-to-earth executive I've ever worked for. But when she asks, you'd better have your answers, your numbers, and your recommendations ready." She does not exempt herself from this kind of rigor. "Meg lives to make crisp, fast-moving decisions," says former Bain colleague-turned-entrepreneur, Scott Cook. "But she [also] listens, she explores, and obsesses about the [eBay] community." This crisis turned eBay from a company vulnerable to technology into a company whose technology, according to Whitman, is a "core competence."[22]

POWER OF COMMUNITY

There was something else that emerged from this e-drama: The strength of the eBay community rose to the forefront. When the site first crashed, eBay expected to be deluged with irate resellers and customers. Instead, just the opposite occurred; people offered support.[23] This attitude is what attracts Whitman to eBay today. "[What] I love about the company is its community of users. It is incredibly fun to see entrepreneurs take advantage of this market-place and utilize it in ways we never would have dreamed."[24] This statement gets to the heart of what eBay really is. It's been called a "global garage sale" (*Christian Science Monitor*) and an "online flea market" (*BusinessWeek, The Economist*), but what eBay really is is a sales outlet for independent businesses, as well as a source for the scarce (tickets to the Super Bowl) to the not-so-scarce—toys and cars—and likely everything in between.

It is also an open door to opportunity for merchants in small towns, as well as megalopolises across the globe, to sell their wares anywhere in the world. eBay is a kind of perfect business; the infrastructure is lean and very electronic. As Whitman once said, "No sales force, no inventory, no warehouses."[25] eBay derives its income from commissions on all sales. It is the middleman between buyers and sellers—but with a crucial difference: It's an auction house. Buyers bid on how much they want to pay. It's Adam Smith economics on steroids, if you will. In this concept there is terrific freedom. The business perpetuates itself and really knows few limits, as Whitman claims, because it is the users who determine what they want to buy and at what price they want to buy it. Sellers dictate content as well as style; they determine trends. In other words, if you want to sell it, they will come.

Of course, there are limits. Technology has its pitfalls, as was seen earlier, but when things are as free and open as they are at eBay, then the unscrupulous will try to take advantage. Every so often people try to scam the system with nonexistent merchandise, as well as ill-gotten gains or other unsavory things, but Whitman contends that "[f]raud is a tiny percentage of the number of [online] listings." One reason for this is that eBay is extremely vigilant, and when it suspects fraud, it acts quickly. The other reason is that the community polices itself, and as a "mainstream shopping destination," the site has earned a reputation for integrity. "eBay is more of an enabler," says Whitman. "We enable, we don't direct." Such self-regulation ensures a degree of security but also the vitality of the marketplace. Its appeal is that you can either sell or buy nearly everything at a price at which you are willing to pay.[26]

HER STORY

Such independence does not come with ease; it comes through diligence, discipline, and commitment. Such attributes also can be applied to Whitman herself. Born into comfortable circumstances, she was a competitive student as well as a competitive athlete, particularly in swimming. Athleticism for young women is almost expected today, but it was less common when Meg was a high school student in the late sixties and seventies. She excelled at Princeton, save for the premed courses, which would have been a problem only if she had her mind set on a career in medicine. Her passion at college was business. She sold advertising for the student paper and later attended Harvard Business School.

Her educational pedigree is enhanced by serving a stint at Procter & Gamble, the proving ground of many successful executives, including Steve Ballmer, CEO of Microsoft. At P&G Meg learned the power of brand—how among the clutter of competing products, brand is the key differential. Later she honed her management skills at Bain & Company, Stride Rite, Walt Disney Company, and FTD, where she learned the value of strategy, as well as what it means to lead an organization.

Her career was not wholly linear. She married a neurosurgeon whom she met at Harvard and had two children. As her children were growing up, she participated in their school and sports activities; yes, she's a soccer mom, too. In fact, she relocated her career for her husband's when he received an offer to work at Massachusetts General Hospital. She became a senior manager at Hasbro toys. Then she received an offer to become the CEO of a small company she had never heard of—eBay.

JOINING EBAY

That offer occurred not without reason. Located in a townhouse, eBay was a fledging Silicon Valley company. Whitman resisted initial overtures, but when she was persuaded to make a visit, she was intrigued by the opportunity. Although small, with 20 employees and annual sales of $4 million, the company was growing exponentially at a compound rate of 70 percent *monthly*.[27] Despite her credentials, when she was interviewed, she did not try to pull rank; she pulled for knowledge. As Omidyar recalled, she made a keen observation that really underscored what eBay was all about. She noted, "It looks like the experience people have with each other helps define your brand."[28]

After agreeing to come aboard, Meg and her family moved back to the West Coast, and she moved into a cubicle in an office of no more than 600 square feet. She continued her learning curve; for the first year and a half, she worked hand in hand with Omidyar, getting to know all she could about the company and at the same time launching its first marketing plan and providing critical insights into growth. She recruited a high-powered board of directors that included Howard Schultz of Starbucks and Scott Cook, who would later found Intuit. In 1998, she made 75 employees millionaires and herself a billionaire by taking eBay public.[29] It was an important day for her, but she never lost perspective. She phoned her husband with the good news about the public listing and reached him in the operating room. He complimented her, but said, "That's nice, but remember that it's not brain surgery."[30]

True enough, but maintaining a company with a growth curve as steep as a rocket launch is hard work. Training is essential at eBay. As Whitman says, "There is no land-based analog for what eBay does." This means that employees must be trained in the mechanics of the business. At the same time, culture is all-important. The way employees deal with each other reflects the culture of the enterprise. "[C]ommunication and teaching [are] probably the biggest challenge," says Whitman. This is not atypical for any startup enterprise, but it's something that Whitman, herself a veteran of long-established businesses, helped bring to eBay.[31]

An indicator of eBay's impact and influence was the coverage of its tenth anniversary in June 2005. While the company held an event at headquarters for its community of users, business and mainstream media noted the maturation of this e-phenomenon that weathered the dot-com bust to emerge stronger and more robust. Of course, eBay is not like other businesses, but it does have customer issues. For example, it recently upped fees, charging 8 percent on all sales. Many eBay sellers rebelled and dropped out. "We really listen hard, . . . and we try to be responsive to the marketplace." Customer service was improved, and the monthly fee for April 2005 was suspended, but the new fee structure remained in place. "It's a bit like citizens in the United States. You make your point of view known. You hope there will be changes." Whitman believes that most eBay sellers will stick with the enterprise. As she says, eBay is "still the best place in the world to start a new business."[32]

SUSTAINING CHARACTER AND CULTURE

Success has brought Meg Whitman recognition; she is routinely named as one of *Fortune* magazine's most powerful women. But it has not gone to her head; she keeps a hardhat in her cubicle to remind her of the terrible days in June 1999 when eBay crashed. She also knows that eBay is not invincible. In 2004, it had to pull out of Japan because it was "a distant no. 2"; being savvy, it deployed its resources to other parts of Asia, Europe, and Latin America to much greater success.[33]

Some of what shaped Meg Whitman's leadership came from her parents. Her mother told her never to listen to stereotypical admonitions such as, "You're not smart enough," "It's a dumb idea," and "Girls don't do that." Her father admonished her to "Be nice to people" when as a 10-year-old she had been nasty. In addition to giving her the standard warning that she may cross paths with someone she had slighted, he added a more telling comment: "You don't change anything by being mean. Usually you don't get anywhere."[34]

This is advice she has lived by. For example, she often flies commercial airlines, and in airports she meets the people who make eBay tick—her customers. They often reveal their "feedback rating" to her as a badge of honor. Whitman understands their pride. After all, as she notes, eBay is a company that measures itself against the highest standards.[35] While Whitman has a résumé that says, "been there and done that," and certainly has enough money for her grandchildren, one thing that keeps her at the helm of eBay is the challenge of creating "something that hasn't been done before" with "the kind of company culture I always wanted to work in."[36] You get a glimpse that this culture is alive and well on the eBay corporate Web page. It says, in part, "Our people are the reason we've come this far. And the reason we'll succeed tomorrow. . . . [W]e'll try our darndest to retain the fun, the community feeling that makes eBay so unique."

Leadership Lessons

- *Be curious.* Leaders must be curious. Meg Whitman is a self-motivated learner who wants to know what is happening and why.
- *Set clear expectations.* People need to know what is expected of them. Whitman sets high expectations for her team but abides by those same high standards for herself.
- *Do not pull rank.* When Meg Whitman joined eBay, she was an accomplished executive, but she did not flout her credentials. She engaged in the business as a peer and learned from the experience.
- *Turn adversity into opportunity.* When disaster struck eBay, Whitman helped to mastermind the reorganization of the company and made technology a pillar of strength for the company.
- *Be humble.* Despite her stature and her wealth, Meg Whitman works in a cubicle and stays connected to her people and her customers.
- *Live for balance.* Meg Whitman is a wife, mother, and CEO. She is engaged in the lives of her family, as well as in the enterprise of her business.

"Whenever I have a movie coming out, I am the same nervous blob of misshapen Jell-O I was when I first began showing those little 8-millimeter films to teeny audiences. That hasn't changed, and it's a very good thing, because I think all of us do our best work when we're the most frightened."[1]

Steven Spielberg

TEACHING YOUR OWN RESULTS-DRIVEN STORY

*R*ARELY DOES IT HAPPEN THAT A COMPANY BECOMES THE DARLING *of the business community, the consulting community, and its own employees, but when it does happen, stories become legion. Consider these stories:*[2]

- *The airline captain who helps the baggage handlers unload when the plane is running late.*

- *The ticket agent who spies a forlorn-looking elderly man alone at the gate. He's missed the last flight, so the agent buys him a meal, puts him up in a hotel, and gets him on the next flight in the morning. She foots the bill.*

- *The culture of pot-luck parties and celebrations for all manner of things from holidays to milestones.*

- *The community-service projects taken on by employees in cities the airline serves.*

- *The former secretary of the cofounder who is now the CEO herself.*

None of these stories should comes as a great surprise, because the energizing force of the company and chairman is a larger-than-life character who is an inveterate people person, "prankster," and all-around good guy. Once he arm-wrestled a CEO to get rights to an advertising slogan.[3] And when asked if he would give up smoking because he had been diagnosed with prostate cancer, he replied, "I don't smoke with my prostate." Character, you bet. Stories, in spades!

Southwest Airlines and its cofounder, Herb Kelleher, are icons in the industry. Southwest was only one of two airlines to see revenues rise in the wake of 9/11. The company is managed by business professionals who invest in their people. They hire for attitude; they train for excellence. They understand and exemplify that people are the most valuable resource. And they celebrate their culture with parties and service awards, and they talk up their culture—so much so that others want to work there and management authors want to write them up. The formula is working; the company is successful and profitable.[4]

And in one final tribute to Herb, the company is doing all of this after he retired from day-to-day responsibilities. Southwest

Airlines sets the standards for others to follow. And the company has the stories to prove it.

The challenge of any leader is to bring people along on the leadership journey. Herb Kelleher excelled in this endeavor literally and figuratively; he traveled extensively to meet with his people, and he constantly communicated the virtues of teamwork and customer service. Two of the best ways that leaders such as Kelleher bring their people with them are through *teaching* and *storytelling*. In fact, good teachers are natural storytellers, and good stories have morals or lessons from which we can learn. Let's take them one at a time.

TEACHING FOR RESULTS

Something remarkable has happened at the Army's Command and General Staff College in Fort Leavenworth, Kansas. Students are teaching. The *Wall Street Journal* reported that officers returning from Afghanistan and Iraq are teaching their classmates and instructors, too, how to fight counterinsurgency conflicts known as *fourth-generation warfare.*[5] The U.S. Army has a long history of applied learning. In fact, there is an entire facility named the Center for Lessons Learned that contains everything from after-action reports of battles to strategic analyses of wars. The purpose is straightforward—to learn from mistakes in order to avoid repeating them.

Those in the private sector can learn from this model of teaching. Successful leaders are essentially teachers. Noel Tichy, a noted author and professor at the University of Michigan business school, has written extensively on the concept of leader–teachers. In *The Leadership Engine*, Tichy promotes the concept of the "teachable moment," where managers find opportunities to impart what they know.[6] Some of teaching that occurs

in companies is prompted by foul-ups. Rather than exacting retribution, enlightened managers turn such foul-ups into instruc-
tional opportunities that enable them to teach and employees to
learn. The message is that we need change, and the hoped-for
outcome is improvement for individuals and the organization.

The concept of leader as teacher is timeless. Our ancient
ancestors were teachers. Men taught boys to fish, hunt, and fight
enemies. Women taught girls to gather food and prepare it for
cooking, along with caring for children and the sick. There were
no lesson plans, nor a curriculum; there was only example. And
example is really the heart of teaching in management. There are
two applications. First, managers adopt what professor Tichy
calls the "teachable point of view," that is, developing things
(issues, problems, solutions) to teach, and when they arise, teach
them. Second, managers who teach set a positive example for
others to follow. This is one way to facilitate the development of
a learning organization where men and women throughout the
enterprise learn from one another and teach what they have
learned to others.[7] Communication is essential to effective
teaching, and here are ways to put communication to work.

- *Make learning a priority.* So much of management is
  applied administration. That is, managers are charged
  with throughput—getting things done—often quickly
  and under pressure. Most managers feel that the workload is so great that to suggest that they devote time to
  teaching seems not merely ridiculous but otherworldly.
  The truth is just the opposite. When managers make time
  to teach, they are preparing others to do some of their
  work. In this way, managers will have more time to
  support their people in getting the work done. Teaching
  becomes an enabling behavior.

- *Look for opportunities to teach.* Teaching within an organizational framework is about creating an environment where
  people can learn. The most obvious lessons come from
  mistakes. For example, if a marketing plan fails, do a post-

mortem to find out why. Analyze each phase to determine what went wrong. Did we fail to identify the correct target? Did our advertising match our brand promise? Did we time our sales launch with our marketing launch? Questions such as these will uncover clues that singly or collectively will provide answers. The key in teaching is not to stop there. Ask why things went right as well as wrong. Then, like a good teacher, challenge the employees to offer alternatives. Such a step-by-step analysis is an exercise that can be repeated often for successes as well as failures.

- *Participate in programs.* Many of the most successful corporate leadership programs involve managers as teachers. General Electric's Crotonville Leadership Development Center popularized this trend, with Jack Welch participating in workout sessions where managers gathered to address problems and find solutions. In essence, it is a variant of the military's practice of after-action review, where officers get together to review things gone wrong, things gone right, and things that can be improved. Many other civilian organizations have followed this same model. When managers act as faculty, they not only learn to become more adept presenters, ones who can orate as well as take questions, but they also gain mastery over their material. Their example also serves as a role model for others; young employees who want to move up quickly learn that teaching is an avenue of development. Over time, organizations develop a culture where teaching is an expected behavior.

- *Teacher as coach.* Management demands enabling others to succeed. What better way is there to ensure success than coaching, which is a form of teaching. Watch a basketball team in action; the coach is directing traffic on the floor, but when players come in from the court, they often huddle with an assistant coach to get an on-the-spot review of their play. In this type of coaching, the instruction is one to one and tailored specifically to the individual. The same can apply in management. Coach-teachers can do more than instruct; they can nudge, cajole, and challenge their employees as a means of pushing them to succeed. Also, they can be there for feedback and follow-up.

MAKING A POSITIVE DIFFERENCE

Even with all the benefits that teaching offers, some managers may resist doing it. Most often they are afraid (alas, mistakenly) that they will not be up to the task. One reason for this fear is that they equate teaching with a classroom lecture. Sometimes it is, but within a corporate environment, the most effective teaching is what occurs on the job. This is why it is important for senior leaders to demonstrate that teaching is every manager's responsibility. For those at the top, the classroom may be the best way to reach the most people; for the middle manager, teaching can occur in coaching sessions or in everyday situations. The only requirement for this to occur is a willingness to try.

Teaching is a vital leadership behavior. It is how leaders prepare the next generation of employees to do what they do, only better. Therefore, teaching is a development exercise for the manager to teach what she knows and therefore develop greater competencies, as well as for employees to learn from people who know how to do things well. A culture of learning develops, which, in the manner of a rising tide lifting all boats, benefits everyone in the organization. Such a culture avoids repeating mistakes and thereby pushes itself to achieve more inspired, and more lasting, results.

TELLING STORIES FOR RESULTS

A second way that leaders bring their followers along is through storytelling. Good leaders can be good storytellers. Stories are the substance of good communication. As I have noted, stories lend context and texture, color and warmth; in short, they resonate with the human side of the enterprise.

Many great leaders, past and present, have been good story-tellers. Lyndon Johnson used to regale his cronies with tales of the Texas Hill Country partly as entertainment and partly as a way of reminding himself of where he came from. In fact, his political mentor, Sam Rayburn, as Speaker of the House, used to hold court in his office with his political colleagues at the end of each business day. Breaking out the branch water, they would chew over the issues of the day. Rayburn called it the "Board of Education." Young Lyndon Johnson learned his lessons at the feet of the master.[8]

CHARACTER IS ACTION

When it comes to creating and telling stories, it is useful to consider the maxim of good drama: Character drives action. In drama, this means that people will act out of a need to do something. In business, this means that people will perform because it is what is expected of them. This concept works well when thinking about stories of organizations in crisis or those undergoing transformation. Leaders rise to challenges; there is something inside of them that compels them to act. Leadership in this instance is not confined to the boardroom; it is everywhere. Consider the customer service employee who personally delivers a needed part to a customer's doorstep, the salesperson who works after hours to help a customer with a display, or the service technician who works overtime on a customer's premises to fix a problem. These kinds of examples happen every day in organizations large and small. They attest to the character of individuals, as well as to the character of the organization, when they are expressed as stories for all to hear and from which to learn.

CREATING YOUR STORY

The leadership journey may represent a single story line—the drive for results. However, the journey itself may be peopled with many individual stories, as I have illustrated throughout this book. However, when creating your own story, it may be useful to examine a variety of story lines. The chief consideration for a story should be its ability to convey the leader's point of view and help the leader bring the followers along in order to fulfill the vision. The story should contain the central purpose of leadership—to achieve desired and inspired results!

As we have seen, stories emerge from everywhere. Steven Spielberg has devoted a lifetime to putting his favorite stories on the screen; he also has created a story of his own by raising a family, building a company, and holding fast to his values, which he imparts in his work as well as in his enterprise. In organizations, stories emerge from people doing something. In mythology, stories emerge from people trying to explain the unexplained. Heroic stories emerge from people getting outside themselves to do something grand, something that makes things better for the organization.

- *Identify a topic.* Look around to find out what people are doing now or what they have done in the past that merits mention. These topics can be about reaching a milestone or about the process of finding ways to reach the milestone.

- *Shape the story: beginning, middle, end.* Describe the situation, the context of the story, that is, what was happening or not happening. Talk about how your heroes decided to do something—fix a problem, propose a solution, or reach out to a customer. Talk about what they did and how what they did changed lives.

- *Find learning lessons.* Emphasize what people learned by doing what they did. How did they grow as individuals or as a team and thereby help the organization grow? Don't be afraid to talk about shortcomings, especially if they result in improvement. This is how we learn.

- *Exemplify the organizational values.* Find the link between what people accomplished and your vision and strategic intentions. Describe how what people did demonstrates their commitment to purpose as well as mission, culture, and values. Sometimes the story will be less about *what* people did and more about *how* they did it—with honor, integrity, and respect for others.

- *Deliver the story.* Consider the story to be an example of good news, and look for all kinds of opportunities to deliver. You can tell it at all-employee meetings or weekly staff gatherings. Don't forget to relate good news to customers. Suppliers, too, need to be considered. You want everyone in your organization to know the successes as well as what they can do to keep the successes coming.

- *Market the story.* Post the story on the Web site or print it in the newsletter. Send an e-mail around the organization letting people know that it's there and what's on it. After you have a number of hero stories, bind them into a collection and distribute it throughout the organization. Give it to key stakeholders: employees, customers, shareholders, and the media. (*Hint*: Create a special hero section on the Web site reserved for stories.)

STORIES WITH METRICS

Stories emphasized throughout this book are narratives—the who, what, why, where, and how of what people did. This mantra is the core of good storytelling, but you can develop and teach stories (as mentioned in Chapter 8) with metrics related to sales quotas, quality increments, and other measurables. In this regard, numbers may tell the story. For example, if the sales team wants to reach sales of $10 million per quarter, post the number on the bulletin board and track progress toward the quota. This is a story. Likewise, when marking improved quality or improved customer service, images of new products (or the product itself) or images of satisfied customers tell the story. Post them on the Web site or bring them into the office space. The demonstration of the achievement is the story.

STORIES, STORIES, STORIES

Leadership communication is the nexus between leadership and communication. Its messages are about things of significance to people because they are involved with vision, alignment, execution, and discipline. The messages resonate more clearly when they are expressed in the form of stories. Stories add meaning because they reflect what people did to overcome an obstacle, achieve a goal, or fulfill a promise. They transcend facts and numbers. They add life to the organization because they are of the organization. Stories reflect the culture of the leaders and followers in the organization. As such, they are personal as well as public. Some stories reflect mistakes; more designate success. They can be uplifting, funny, piquant, and powerful. They are stories about people who made a difference, and for that, the stories are to be remembered and told and retold. Leadership is the act of persuading people to follow, and what better way is there to do it than with stories.

Stories propel the leadership journey. Look for them. Create them. Tell them. Distribute them. And tell them again and again. Stories exemplify who we are as individuals and what we can become as visionaries, aligners, executors, disciplinarians, risk-takers, and result-makers—in short, leaders of ourselves, our teams, and our organizations.

Your Own Results Story Planner

Stories exist throughout your organization. There is the big story, of course, about what it takes to achieve the vision. But there are many other small but important stories that arise and reside in the actions of what your people are doing to keep focused, aligned, executing, and disciplined. It is the leader's responsibility to capture and publicize the stories as a means of bringing people along on the leadership journey. Use the following questions to help develop these stories.

- What do you want to tell people?
- Who in your organization exemplifies this message?
- What events have occurred recently that you can use to create context for the story?
- What happened first?
- What happened next?
- What do you want people to remember about your story?
- How should you tell this story, that is, in a speech, at a meeting, on a bulletin, in a newsletter, or on the Web?

STEVEN SPIELBERG

The opening credits of *Amazing Stories,* a television anthology series that lasted two seasons in the mid-1980s, give a glimpse into the mind of one our era's greatest storytellers. The opening frames reveal a tribal elder positioned near an open fire in a cave. In word and gesture we presume that the man is spinning a tale about his people. The story may be religious or ritualistic or simply a good yarn about a recent hunt. We cannot tell, but what we can know is that the story is enthralling and creates a connection to all who witness it. The man behind *Amazing Stories* is Steven Spielberg. While the series was not a major point on his screen résumé, it does provide insight into the power of story, as well as into why Spielberg has devoted his life to telling stories of every kind on the big screen. From his first blockbuster movie, *Jaws,* to the more recent *War of the Worlds*, and so many other memorable pictures in between such as *E.T.;* the Indiana Jones series; *Minority Report; A.I.;* and, of course, *Schindler's List* and *Saving Private Ryan*, Steven Spielberg has created an indelible mark on the history of American cinema. And in doing so he has created a legacy of stories from which any manager can learn and draw lessons.

FROM THE BEGINNING

Steven Spielberg has always wanted to be a movie director. At the age of 8, he began making movies. By the time he was 15, he had won an award. And by age 22, he had gained a seven-year contract with Universal Pictures, the kind they used to give to actors. His first professional assignment was a television episode for an anthology series, *Night Gallery;* the star was Joan Crawford. He admits that he was in over his head, but he had planned every shot in advance, and so he was ready. The only problem was that he was calling for 15 setups on the first day. He accomplished only half of them, but he made it through because he threw himself on the mercy of the crew, who bailed him out. It is not a lesson he has forgotten.[9]

It is worth noting that Spielberg collects Norman Rockwell paintings. "Aside from being an astonishing good storyteller," Spielberg points out, "Rockwell spoke volumes about a certain kind of American morality." As journalist Stephen Dubner put it, Spielberg could be defining himself with such a description. Spielberg claims never to have made an "immoral film" or one he was not proud of in a sense of "leading people astray." He is the *ur*-entertainment director. While some critics may scoff, this ability in his films "to please people" is a gift. It has brought him immense wealth, as well as immense influence. Surprisingly, however, Spielberg does not let it go to his head. He decries the term *mogul* and is respectful of other talents; he remains rooted in the present despite a soaring ambition to continue his life's calling.[10]

Morality is evident in *E.T.*, his admitted favorite. The story revolves around a little boy who lives a solitary life until he encounters an alien, whom he befriends. His adventure opens him to real life and improved relations with family and friends. *The Color Purple* was Spielberg's first "serious film." The movie is based on an Alice Walker novel and deals with the dark themes of racial prejudice and rape. Spielberg bonded with the story but wasn't certain that he was the right person to direct it because he isn't black. To this, Quincy Jones, noted composer and a producer on the film, replied, "You didn't have to come from Mars to do *E.T.,* did you?" Jones urged Spielberg to direct the film because "[he] loved [the story] more than anyone else."[11]

Spielberg often has been labeled as a director of "big-concept films." It is a label about which he is not wholly comfortable. "I've always felt that all of my films were personal," says Spielberg, "because I've never made a film where some part of the story didn't come from some experience I shared with my family." David Brode, author of *The Films of Steven Spielberg,* agrees: "He gives the public what they want while slipping in what he wants. He's having it both ways." A strong theme in Spielberg's personal vision is optimism, even when making movies about aliens. "My heart will always look up into the sky and feel optimistic about what's out there."[12]

"Popcorn movies"—Spielberg's term to describe movies such as *Raiders of the Lost Ark* and the Jurassic Park series—give him the financial freedom to experiment.[13] More recently, he has explored the dark side of technology and what it portends for the future in *A.I.,* a film about robots taking over; *Minority Report,* about what happens when government becomes too intrusive; and *War of the Worlds,* about frightfully powerful technology used by aliens to destroy Earth. But two films stand out—at least to date—as testaments to his values and ability to tell a powerful story, as the next section shows.

EXPRESSING THE HEART AND SOUL

Schindler's List was a film 10 years in the making. A bit of Hollywood bravado, but not! This is the time frame that Spielberg gave Poldek Pfefferberg, one of the 1,100 Jews that Schindler saved and who told his story to Thomas Kenneally, who was intrigued enough to write the nonfiction novel telling the story of a charmer, conniver, debaucher, but righteous man who braved the odds and turned a buck and saved Jews from the Nazi death machine. For

Spielberg, it was not a matter of production; it was a matter of courage—of telling the story the way it should be told. True to his word, Spielberg began making the movie on location in Auschwitz and other Polish locales. To shoot this movie in black and white for a mere $22 million, Spielberg put on his game face and worked quickly, dispensing for the most part with swooping crane angles and complicated dolly shots, instead opting for the realism of hand-held footage. In one scene, the actors playing Jews were required to run wild through the streets because they were being chased; the emotion and pain was evident in the re-creation. Some scenes, such as the ones of naked old people running in circles to prove their fitness before the Nazi guards, were too realistic for Spielberg to watch, even though it was a staged event for the cameras. Anger surfaced as he made the film, not tears.

The film's complexity derives from Schindler and his relationship with Amon Goeth, the vulgar Nazi officer who ran the camp, and Schindler himself, who wants to make a profit at the same time he wants to save people. Eventually, his true goodness triumphs over his quest for riches, but the moral equation lies close the surface of the film. For Spielberg, it was a triumph. The film earned more than $320 million and gained Spielberg his first Oscar. It also marked a transition from the maker of light entertainment to the maker of serious drama.[14]

World War II provided the backdrop for Spielberg's next epic, *Saving Private Ryan,* about a company of soldiers ordered to find the sole surviving son (eligible for exemption from combat) who is serving as an Army private somewhere in Normandy. The plot may be melodramatic (with some basis in fact), but the circumstance is harrowing. After a prologue that takes place in a cemetery for U.S. soldiers in present-day France, Spielberg brings us to the assault on Omaha Beach. Never before on the big screen has the sheer hell of a frontal assault on a heavily fortified position been so authentically depicted. In shot after shot, through graphic images and hair-raising sound effects, the audience feels some semblance of what it must have been like on that fateful morning in June 1944 when the Allies began tenuously but determinedly to take back Europe from the tyranny of Nazism. The power of the film derives not from the grand themes of freedom but from the all-too-human dramas of soldiers who do their duty not as much for God and country as for—what historian Stephen Ambrose (also an adviser on the film) wrote so eloquently about—their buddies in the same unit. Again, this film brought honors to Spielberg and demonstrated the power of his ability to tell a story simply and searingly.

In the wake of the populist movie *War of the Worlds*, Spielberg again demonstrated his willingness to deal with tough topics. His newest film, slated for general release in 2006, concerns the Israeli reaction to the assassinations of 11 of its athletes at the 1972 Munich Olympics. In the wake of the attack, Mossad struck back by killing as many of the perpetrators as it could. It is a film certain to stir dark memories and deep passions in Israel. In a statement about the film, Spielberg referred to the attack and the Israeli response as "a defining moment in the history of the Middle East." Spielberg sought guidance on script development from former high-ranking U.S. government officials. "What comes through [in the script] is the human dimension," said Donald Ross, who served as a Middle East envoy for former President Clinton.

Spielberg's statement puts the film in context: "Viewing Israel's response to Munich through the eyes of the men who were sent to avenge that tragedy adds a human dimension to a horrific episode that we usually think about only in political or military terms. By experiencing how the implacable resolve of these men to succeed in their mission slowly gave way to troubling doubts about what they were doing, I think we can learn something important about the tragic standoff we find ourselves in today." In a story about the new film, the *New York Times* cited a statement made by Golda Meir, who was Israel's prime minister at the time. "It's easy to look back at historic events with the benefit of hindsight," said Meir. "What's not so easy is to try to see things as they must have looked to people at the time."

Gaining perspective on that tragic period is something that gifted storytellers like Spielberg excel in doing.[15]

ATTENTION TO DETAIL

As a director, Spielberg is notoriously well prepared. The production of his movies is crisp, clean, and efficient. There is little waste. For example, during the making of *Saving Private Ryan*, the set builders mistakenly built a set facing into the sun. Most directors would have razed it. Not Steven. He engaged his imagination and with his cameraman came up with new shooting angles to exploit the design, not abolish it. This is one reason the war epic was made for $65 million, which is a fraction of the $200 million plus that the movie *Titanic* cost. Such cost control indicates a director who is well in control of his craft, his team, and his ego.[16]

Naturally, you don't get to where Spielberg is today without a keen sense of business acumen. In 1998, *The Economist* reported that of the 16 feature films that Spielberg had directed, 13 had turned a profit; add one more for *Saving Private Ryan* (released that year), and you have a track record that defies odds. The average rate of films turning a profit in Hollywood is one in three. (As of 2005 and prior to the release of *War of the Worlds*, his films have grossed $3.2 billion, nearly twice as much as any other single director.) Spielberg has had his own production company since early in his career, but in 1994, together with record producer David Geffen and movie producer Jeffrey Katzenberg, he formed DreamWorks SKG. Based on their proven abilities, the principals were able to raise $2.7 billion in investment capital. Initial productions were far from hits—its first television series, its first music release, and its first movie release, *Amistad*, did not fare well.[17] However, since that time, fortunes have improved. The company has produced successful animated features such as *Prince of Egypt*, *Antz,* and the two *Shreks*. Spielberg has returned to television by producing prime-time shows and extended miniseries such as *Taken* for the SciFi Channel and *Into the West* for TNT. Like all entertainment companies, DreamWorks SKG has ventured into video games. In the summer of 2005, Universal bought the live-action movie unit of DreamWorks SKG. In doing so it gained important movie properties including *Gladiator* and *American Beauty,* as well as the right to distribute DreamWorks animation features. According to the *Wall Street Journal,* this purchase demonstrates how difficult it is to create and maintain a major independent studio in an era of declining movie revenues and domination by six major studios, Universal being one of them.[18] It also demonstrates that Spielberg remains a savvy businessman; no sense holding a property when it cannot deliver a viable return on investment.

GIVING BACK

What does one do with all that money, influence, and success? If you are Steven Spielberg, you give back. First, he actively supports the work of young filmmakers. He has jump-started the career of many first-time directors, among them Robert Zemeckis. He is also very supportive of women in film. Two of his former secretaries are producers; one of them, Kathleen Kennedy, has served as producer on many of his directorial efforts.[19]

Family is very important to Spielberg. He grew up in a household with his mother, Leah, to whom he is still very close, and his three sisters. It was a household he once described as a "suburban psychodrama," characterizing his experience as "[g]rowing up in a family with three screaming younger sisters and a mother who played concert piano with seven other women."[20] After his parents divorced when he was a teenager, he pulled away from his father, Arnold, a computer engineer. They later reunited. Steven credits his father with supporting his early moviemaking, as well as with educating him about World War II. (Arnold was a radio operator on B-25s.) Spielberg is father to seven children, one from his first marriage to actress Amy Irving and five with actress Kate Capshaw, who brought an adult daughter into their marriage.[21]

Faith is another constant in his life. Although he grew up Jewish, at times Orthodox—even when he wanted Christmas lights so that he wouldn't appear different from other kids—he was not observant as a young adult. Age and having his own children changed his outlook. He and wife, Kate, are now what he calls "time-permitting practitioners of Judaism." More important, he lives his faith. It is what compelled him to make *Schindler's List* and what has propelled him, in part, to philanthropy. He confesses that he once proudly gave away a great deal of money with his name attached. But a rabbi pulled him aside and said, "You know, if you put your name on everything, it goes unrecognized by God." Taking the advice to heart, Spielberg now makes most donations anonymously, only attaching his "name [to] help attract other moneys." Two causes dear to him are the Shoah Foundation and the Righteous Persons Foundation. The latter was begun with "profits from *Schindler's List*." As he puts it, "I was unwilling to keep it because it was blood money."[22]

What Steven Spielberg will do next depends on personal preference. After all, he is a former Boy Scout, but one who admitted to the *New York Times* that he wasn't always living up to the organization's values. He says, comparing himself to the credo, "I'm trustworthy. I'm loyal. I'm sometimes friendly. I'm always courteous, not always kind, not always obedient, not always cheerful, mostly thrifty as a producer, not brave at all, always clean, and *very* reverent."[23] He has the resources and drawing power to produce anything on the screen he wants. But you can bet that like all successful Hollywood moguls, it will be the story that attracts his attention and compels him to devote a year or more to putting that story into a form that will delight, enthrall, educate, and entertain millions of moviegoers. And that's quite a story.

Leadership Lessons

- *Think big.* Steven Spielberg lives to put stories on the big screen. Whether it is an epic or a sci-fi fantasy or anything in between, Spielberg adds a larger-than-life dimension to his stories that makes them accessible as well as compelling.

- *Control your destiny.* Spielberg has parlayed his success into production agreements in film and television that give him the control to put his vision, as well as the dreams of many fellow directors, into digital and celluloid realities.

- *Work in a team.* Making a movie or running a production house is a cooperative enterprise. Spielberg has surrounded himself with men and women who share his commitment so that he can pursue his passion of making stories come alive.

- *Share the credit.* Actors like to work with Spielberg because he gives them the freedom to create the rich dimensions of their characters. And he is always first to extol their virtues.

- *Live your values.* While his body of work ranges from sci-fi to suspense, comedy to war, and more, Steven Spielberg is a man who is generous with his time to promote good causes as well as create new awareness of social issues. The strength of his character radiates to the screen.

APPENDIX

ACHIEVING RESULTS FOR YOUR PEOPLE

Leadership is about achieving inspired results the right way. This means doing what is right and good for individuals and teams in order to build trust and get things done on time, on budget, and with the support of others. Achieving lasting results can be an arduous task, and it often calls for tough decisions. It may not always work this way. Sometimes, organizational goals must supersede those of individuals, but where possible, strive to put the needs of people first. Here are some suggestions:

Communicate the Vision

- Think big.
- Focus the vision.
- Describe the vision in real terms.
- Provide the "What's in it for me?" (WIFM).
- Sell the vision.
- Communicate the vision in personal terms.
- Hold vision off-sites.
- Create vision maps.
- Tell vision stories.

Create Alignment

- Emphasize mission.
- Describe strategies.
- Link steps with actions.
- Establish milestones.
- Keep the plan flexible.
- Do a team gut check.

Execute Flawlessly

- Take action steps.
- Manage teams.
- Follow up.
- Lead by letting go.
- Create opportunities for fulfillment.

Exert Discipline

- Reinforce organizational goals.
- Insist on accountability.
- Evaluate regularly.
- Provide coaching.

Take Responsible Risks

- Assess opportunities and risks.
- Think outside the box.
- Value creativity.
- Push innovation.
- Consider the "visionary risk."
- Consider the return on risk.

Demonstrate Courage

- Value courage.

- Publicize courage.

- Tell stories of courage.

- Have the courage to postpone immediate gain for a better future.

- Assess fear in the organization.

- Proliferate courage.

Celebrate Results

- Mark milestones.

- Celebrate achievements.

- Recognize the contributors.

- Demonstrate engagement.

- Sustain results.

- Create the value equation.

ACHIEVING RESULTS FOR YOURSELF

Organizational results flow from individual results. You must have the desire as well as the will to want to make a positive difference for yourself and the organization. Toward that end, you must be willing to implement some of the same things we ask organizations to do. Organizations reflect the collective will of their people, and that will begins with one person at a time. Here are some suggestions to help you achieve results in your own life:

Communicate the Vision

- Think of what you can achieve in line with your personal vision.

- Apply your vision to the organizational vision.
- Describe what fulfillment of the vision will mean to you.

Create Alignment

- Examine what you do in relation to what others do.
- Consider how you manage others according to the mission.
- Act in accordance with vision and mission.
- Create personal milestones.
- Do a gut check.

Execute Flawlessly

- Act for the benefit of the team.
- Manage for the benefit of the organization.
- Follow up with everyone.

Exert Discipline

- Hold yourself accountable.
- Ask for feedback from others.
- Insist on coaching for yourself.

Take Responsible Risks

- Assess personal opportunities and personal risks.
- Challenge yourself to think differently.
- Put yourself out of the comfort zone.

Demonstrate Courage

- Assess your own fears.
- Believe in your abilities.

- Have faith in your convictions.

- Read hero stories.

- Apply lessons of hero stories to yourself and your team.

Celebrate Results

- Acknowledge your own contributions.

- Look for ways to keep pushing forward.

- Look for ways to sustain your energy and momentum.

- Take time for yourself (regularly).

LEADERSHIP STORY MODEL

Leadership Process		Communication Action
Vision	→	Visualizing and verbalizing where the organization needs to go
Alignment	→	Describing the steps the organization needs to take to fulfill the vision
Execution	→	Transforming action steps into accomplishments
Discipline	→	Advising, prodding, and coaching
Risk	→	Encouraging people to act "out of the box" in order to fulfill the vision
Courage	→	Standing up for beliefs and convictions that help achieve intended results
Results	→	Recognizing the contributions of others

Endnotes

PROLOGUE

[1] Warren G. Bennis and Burt Nanus, *Leaders: Strategies for Taking Charge*, 2d ed. New York: Harper Business, 2003, p. 20.

[2] U. S. Grant, *Personal Memoirs of U. S. Grant*, with a new introduction by William S. McFeeley. New York: DaCapo Press/Plenum Press, 1982.

CHAPTER 1

[1] Tom Walsh, "Ghosn's Vision Motivates Staff, Delivers Results," *Detroit Free Press*, January 18, 2005.

[2] Adapted from William Lee Miller, *Lincoln's Virtues, an Ethical Biography*. New York: Vintage Books, 2002, p. 174.

[3] Abraham Lincoln and Donald T. Phillips, *Lincoln's Stories for Leaders*. Arlington, TX: Summit Publishing Group, 1997, pp. 35–36.

[4] Spencer E. Ante, "Online Extra: Autodesk: 'We're the 'It' Company,'" *Business Week 50—Tech Outlook*, April 4, 2005.

[5] Carol Bartz, "Engineering a Solution: Bring Women into the Fold," *San Jose Mercury News*, March 24, 2005.

[6] Lee Gomes, "Picking New Strategy? Getting on Right Side of History Can Be Key," *Wall Street Journal*, April 4, 2005.

[7] Facts about Autodesk's businesses, annual revenues, global distribution, and market size come from its Web site: www.autodesk.com .

[8] Gregory H. Patton, "The Business Case for Communication Skills Development," [unpublished] citing 2002–2004 *Wall Street Journal/ Harris Interactive* poll written by Stewart Alsop, 2005.

[9] Nick Morgan, *Working the Room: How to Move People to Action through Audience-Centered Speaking*. Boston: Harvard Business School Press, 2003, pp. 61–64.

[10] "Face Value: The $10 Billion Man," *The Economist*, February 26, 2005.

[11] Ibid.; David Magee, *Turnaround: How Carlos Ghosn Rescued Nissan*. New York: Harper Business, 2003, pp. 15–34.

[12] David Magee, *Turnaround: How Carlos Ghosn Rescued Nissan*. New York: Harper Business, 2003, pp. 29–43.

[13] Alex Taylor, interview with Carlos Ghosn, "Advice from a Fellow Outsider," *Fortune*, April 4, 2005.

[14] David Magee, *Turnaround: How Carlos Ghosn Rescued Nissan*. New York: Harper Business, 2003, pp. 44–65.

[15] Ibid., pp. 66–85, 96–97.

[16] Ibid., pp. 138–143, 178–179.

[17] Ibid., pp. 190–191.

[18] Ibid., pp. 73–79, 175–178.

[19] Jo Wrighton and Jathon Sapsford, "Split Shift: For Nissan's Rescuer, Ghosn, New Road Rules Await at Renault," *Wall Street Journal*, April 26, 2005.

[20] David Magee, *Turnaround: How Carlos Ghosn Rescued Nissan*. New York: Harper Business, 2003, pp. 135–136, 155–158.

[21] Ibid., pp. 147–155.

[22] Ibid., pp. 160–166.

[23] Carlos Ghosn and Phillippe Ries, *Shift: Inside Nissan's Historic Turnaround* (trans. by John Cullen). New York: Currency Books/ Doubleday, 2005, pp. 148–159 (French edition published in 2003).

[24] Ibid., pp. 95, 174–183.

[25] Christine Tierney, "Nissan CEO: The Making of a Superstar," *Detroit News*, February 27, 2005 (quote is from former Nissan executive Jason Vines, now with DaimlerChrysler).

[26] Ibid.

[27] Carlos Ghosn and Phillippe Ries, *Shift: Inside Nissan's Historic Turnaround* (trans. by John Cullen). New York: Currency Books/Doubleday, 2005. p. 131 (French edition published in 2003).

[28] Jo Wrighton and Jathon Sapsford, "Split Shift: For Nissan's Rescuer, Ghosn, New Road Rules Await at Renault," *Wall Street Journal*, April 26, 2005.

[29] Alex Taylor, interview with Carlos Ghosn, "Advice from a Fellow Outsider," *Fortune*, April 4, 2005.

[30] Christine Tierney, "Nissan CEO: The Making of a Superstar," *Detroit News*, February 27, 2005.

CHAPTER 2

[1] "Our DNA Hasn't Changed," *Fortune*, February 6, 2005.

[2] Baltasar Gracian, S.J., *The Art of Worldly Wisdom: 300 Practical Proposals for Success by a 17th Century Jesuit*. Springfield, IL: Templegate Publishers, 1996, p. 24.

[3] Obituary: "Christopher Reeve," *The Economist*, October 16, 2004.

[4] "Reeve Was Real-Life 'Superman,'" Reuters, October 11, 2004.

[5] Obituary: "Christopher Reeve," *The Economist*, October 16, 2004.

[6] Except where noted, biographical facts are drawn from two sources: Douglas Martin, "Christopher Reeve, 52, Symbol of

Courage, Dies," *New York Times*, October 11, 2004; and "Christopher Reeve, 'Superman' Star, Dies at 52," Associated Press, October 11, 2004.

[7] Chris Matthews, Interview with Bob Graham, *Hardball*, May 5, 2005.

[8] Robert Lenzer, "Room at the Top," *Forbes*, April 28, 2003.

[9] Brent Schlender, "Interview with Steve Jobs," *Fortune*, February 7, 2005.

[10] Brent Schlender, "How Big Can Apple Get?" *Fortune*, February 7, 2005.

[11] Neil McIntosh, "No Sleeping on the Jobs," *The Guardian*, September 23, 1999.

[12] "The Obsessiveness of Steve Jobs," *The Economist*, May 7, 2005.

[13] Brent Schlender, "Steve Jobs: The Graying Price of a Shrinking Kingdom," *Fortune*, May 14, 2001.

[14] Brent Schlender, "Interview with Steve Jobs," *Fortune*, February 7, 2005.

[15] Bruce Orwall, "A Beautiful Friendship?—Split between Jobs, Eisner over Digital Piracy Threatens Future Pixar-Disney Deals," *Wall Street Journal*, May 17, 2002.

[16] Devin Leonard, "This Is War," *Fortune*, May 27, 2002.

[17] Brent Schlender, "How Big Can Apple Get?" *Fortune*, February 7, 2005.

[18] Steven Jobs, "Commencement Address at Stanford University delivered June 12, 2005," *Stanford Report* 6/14/05.

[19] Ibid.

[20] Brent Schlender, "Interview with Steve Jobs," *Fortune*, February 7, 2005.

[21] Additional sources include Steven Berglas, "What You Can Learn from Steve Jobs," *Inc Boston*, October 1999; Tobi Elkin and Joan Voight, "Steve Jobs: Return of the King," *Brandweek New York*, October 12, 1998; Henry Norr, "Apple's New Core: Jobs Shifts Company Toward 'Digital Lifestyle' Products," *San Francisco*

Chronicle, January 10, 2001; Henry Norr, "'Second Coming' Attempts to Decode Steve Jobs/Pixar, Applehoncho Analyzed," *San Francisco Chronicle*, October 10, 2001; Josh Quittner, "Apple's New Core," *Time*, January 14, 2002; Roger Ridey, "Network: The Mac Faithful Pin Their Hopes on the Miracle Man," *The Independent* (London), January 8, 2001; and Jon Schwartz, "Jobs as Complex as Citizen Kane, Author Writes," *USA Today*, July 27, 2000.

CHAPTER 3

[1] "Xerox CEO Reveals Her Secrets of Success at Toledo, Ohio, Diversity Forum," *Toledo Blade/Knight Ridder Tribune Business News*, November 13, 2003.

[2] Robyn Meredith with Jonathan Fahey, "The 'Ooof' Company," *Forbes*, April 14, 2003.

[3] Ibid.

[4] Ibid.

[5] Norika Shirouzu and Jathon Sapsford, "For Toyota, a New Small Truck Carries Hope for Topping GM," *Wall Street Journal*, May 12, 2005.

[6] Norihiko Shirouzu, "Toyota Runs Low on Expertise to Power Global Push," *Wall Street Journal*, July 13, 2005.

[7] Tanya Clark, "'Destructive Force': Toyota's Okuda Speaks Out," *Industry Week*, July 6, 1999.

[8] Stephanie N. Mehta, "Pat Russo's Lucent Vision," *Fortune*, March 31, 2002.

[9] Shawn Young, "Leadership: Less May Be More: Lucent Technologies Saw Its Future in Rapid Growth, Then Hit a Wall," *Wall Street Journal*, October 25, 2004.

[10] Larry Kudlow and Jim Cramer, "Lucent Technologies—CEO Interview," CNBC, January 20, 2005.

[11] Stephanie N. Mehta, "Pat Russo's Lucent Vision," *Fortune*, March 31, 2002.

[12] Ibid.

[13] Marcus Buckingham and Curt Coffman, *First, Break All the Rules*. New York: Simon & Schuster, 1999, pp. 72–104.

[14] I would like to thank Marshall Goldsmith, coach, consultant, and author, for his insight into the difference between mission and goals.

[15] John U. Bacon, *America's Corner: Walgreen's Prescription for Success*. Hoboken, NJ: Wiley, 2004.

[16] Betsy Morris, "The Accidental CEO," *Fortune*, June 9, 2003.

[17] Anne M. Mulcahy, with Claudia Deutsch, "Shaped by Family Debates," *New York Times*, October 1, 2001.

[18] Betsy Morris, "The Accidental CEO," *Fortune*, June 9, 2003.

[19] Bill George and Andrew N. McLean, "Anne Mulcahy: Leading Xerox through the Perfect Storm (A)," Harvard Business School business case 9-405-050.

[20] "Xerox CEO Reveals Her Secrets of Success at Toledo, Ohio Diversity Forum," *Toledo Blade/Knight Ridder Tribune Business News*, November 13, 2003.

[21] Betsy Morris, "The Accidental CEO," *Fortune*, June 9, 2003.

[22] Ibid.

[23] Anne Mulcahy, "Lead Your Employees through Hell and Back," *Business 2.0*, December 2002.

[24] Bill George and Andrew N. McLean, "Anne Mulcahy: Leading Xerox through the Perfect Storm (A)," Harvard Business School business case 9-405-050.

[25] Betsy Morris, "The Accidental CEO," *Fortune*, June 9, 2003.

[26] Ibid.

[27] "Xerox CEO Reveals Her Secrets of Success at Toledo, Ohio Diversity Forum," *Toledo Blade/Knight Ridder Tribune Business News*, November 13, 2003.

[28] Susan Roth, "Xerox CEO Proud of Company's Recovery," Gannett News Service, April 2, 2003.

[29] Betsy Morris, "The Accidental CEO," *Fortune*, June 9, 2003.

[30] Bill George and Andrew N. McLean, "Anne Mulcahy: Leading Xerox through the Perfect Storm (A)," Harvard Business School business case 9-405-050.

[31] Diane Brady, "You've Come the Wrong Way Baby," *BusinessWeek*, March 28, 2005.

[32] Anne Mulcahy, "Lead Your Employees through Hell and Back," *Business 2.0*, December 2002; Betsy Morris, "The Accidental CEO," *Fortune*, June 9, 2003.

[33] Bill George and Andrew N. McLean, "Anne Mulcahy: Leading Xerox through the Perfect Storm (A)," Harvard Business School business case 9-405-050.

CHAPTER 4

[1] Louis V. Gerstner, *Who Says Elephants Can't Dance?* New York: Harper Business, 2002, p. 231.

[2] "Red Adair (obituary)," *The Economist*, August 14, 2004.

[3] Christopher Reed, "Obituary: Red Adair: Swashbuckling Troubleshooter Renowned for Taming Huge Oil-Well Fires," *The Guardian* (Manchester, UK), August 9, 2004.

[4] "Showmanship of Famed Houston Oil Firefighter Red Adair Adds to His Legend," *Houston Chronicle/Knight Ridder Tribune Business News*, August 11, 2004.

[5] "Red Adair (obituary)," *The Economist*, August 14, 2004.

[6] Ibid.

[7] "Showmanship of Famed Houston Oil Firefighter Red Adair Adds to His Legend" *Houston Chronicle/Knight Ridder Tribune Business News*, August 11, 2004.

[8] Ibid.

[9] Stewart Alsop, "IBM: Eating My Own Words," *Fortune*, February 3, 2002.

[10] Betsy Morris, "He's Smart. He's Not Nice. He's Saving Big Blue," *Fortune*, April 14, 1997.

[11] Ibid.; Louis V. Gerstner, *Who Says Elephants Can't Dance?* New York: Harper Business, 2002, p. 16.

[12] Betsy Morris, "He's Smart. He's Not Nice. He's Saving Big Blue," *Fortune*, April 14, 1997.

[13] Ibid.

[14] Louis V. Gerstner, *Who Says Elephants Can't Dance?* New York: Harper Business, 2002, pp. 23–25.

[15] Ibid., pp. 68–72.

[16] Ibid., pp. 50–51.

[17] Ibid., pp. 121-127.

[18] Ibid., p. 213.

[19] Ibid., pp. 235–238.

[20] Betsy Morris, "He's Smart. He's Not Nice. He's Saving Big Blue," *Fortune*, April 14, 1997.

[21] Stewart Alsop, "IBM: Eating My Own Words," *Fortune*, February 3, 2002.

CHAPTER 5

[1] David Aldridge, "Belichick's Mantra Is in Midseason Form," *Philadephia Inquirer/Knight Ridder Newspapers*, March 22, 2005

[2] James Tobin, *To Conquer the Air: The Wright Brothers and the Great Race for Flight*. New York: Free Press, 2003, pp. 190–192.

[3] Ibid., p. 347.

[4] Ibid., pp. 293, 313.

[5] Facts and quotes from Curt Schleier, "Executive Ann Fudge: Relies on Lessons of Youth to Keep Business Growing," *Investor's Business*

Daily, June 7,/1999; *Business Leaders & Success*, Introduction by William J. O'Neil. New York: McGraw-Hill, 2004.

[6] Ann Fudge, "Best Advice I Ever Got," *Fortune*, March 31, 2005.

[7] John Baldoni, *Great Motivation Secrets of Great Leaders*. New York: McGraw-Hill, 2005, pp. 51–61.

[8] Pete Thamel, "For Belichick, an Economy of Thought," *New York Times*, January 16, 2004.

[9] Ibid.

[10] Damon Hack, "For Patriot's Coach, War Is Decided before Game," *New York Times*, February 3, 2005.

[11] Ibid.

[12] Ibid.

[13] Judy Battista, "Patriots Adhere to Bottom Line to Stay on Top," *New York Times*, August 8, 2004.

[14] Damon Hack, "For Patriot's Coach, War Is Decided before Game," *New York Times*, February 3, 2005.

[15] Ron Borges, "At Media Breakfast, Belichick Won't Bite," *Boston Globe*, March 23, 2005.

[16] David Aldridge, "Belichick's Mantra Is in Midseason Form," *Philadelphia Inquirer/Knight Ridder Newspapers*, March 22, 2005.

[17] Andy Hart, "There's a Charm for Pats' White House Visits," *Patriots Football Weekly*, April 13, 2005.

[18] Ty Banks, "Here We Go Again," SI.com, August 1, 2005 [Belichick quote on change]; Dave Goldberg, "Patriots in Pursuit of a Three-Peat," Associated Press (*Ann Arbor News*), August 15, 2005 [Brady quote].

[19] "Coach Belichick, Wesleyan Alumnus, Accepts Honorary Degree from his Alma Mater," Press release Wesleyan University. Commencement May 22, 2005. [Note: no date was given for release.]

[20] Steve Mazzone, "Belichick Keynote Speaker at Bryant," *Herald News* (Fall River, MA) Journal Register News Service, April 1, 2005.

CHAPTER 6

1 Paul West, "Michigan's Governor's Race Focuses on a Rising Star," *Baltimore Sun*, September 16, 2002.

2 Daniel Roth, "Nike after Knight," *Fortune*, April 4, 2005.

3 Larry Smith interview with Phil Knight, *CNN Presents: Top 25 Business Leaders*, March 13, 2005.

4 Daniel Roth, "Nike after Knight," *Fortune*, April 4, 2005.

5 Ibid.

6 Melanie Kletter, "Labor Cites Nike Study as Model," *Women's Wear Daily*, April 15, 2005.

7 Daniel Roth, "Nike after Knight," *Fortune*, April 4, 2005.

8 Larry Smith interview with Phil Knight, *CNN Presents: Top 25 Business Leaders*, March 13, 2005.

9 Daniel Roth, "Nike after Knight," *Fortune*, April 4, 2005.

10 "Leonard Tose, a Big Spender" (obituary), *The Economist*, April 24, 2003.

11 Kevin Mulligan, "Tose Goes Out on the Wings of Eagles. Emotional Eulogies Highlight Funeral Services," *Philadelphia Daily News*, April 21, 2003.

12 "Leonard Tose, a Big Spender" (obituary), *The Economist*, April 24, 2003.

13 Bill Breen, "High Stakes, Big Bets," *Fast Company*, April 2002.

14 Ibid.

15 Ibid.

16 Henry Chesbrough, "Reinventing R&D Through Open Innovation," *Strategy + Business eNews*, April 30, 2003.

17 Diane Brady, "The Immelt Revolution," *BusinessWeek*, March 28, 2005.

18 Christine Tierney, "Toyota to Invest $150 Million in Michigan," *Detroit News*, April 13, 2005.

[19] "Jennifer Granholm," *Almanac of American Politics*, October 15, 2003.

[20] Ibid.

[21] Ibid.; Paul West, "Michigan's Governor's Race Focused on Rising Star," *Baltimore Sun*, September 16, 2002.

[22] "Granholm: 40,000 Jobs Can Be Created in Three Years," Associated Press, March 29, 2005.

[23] "Granholm Says Michigan Must 'Eat or Be Eaten' Economically," Associated Press, May 2, 2005.

[24] "Granholm Makes the Case for Selling Bonds to Invest in Job Growth," Associated Press, May 4, 2005.

[25] "Free Press Editorial Board Interview with Jennifer Granholm," *Detroit Free Press*, February 10, 2005.

[26] "Granholm Says Michigan Must 'Eat or Be Eaten' Economically," Associated Press, May 2, 2005.

[27] Louis Aguilar, "Granholm Reiterates Education's Value," *Detroit News*, May 3, 2005; Brian Dickerson, "Bad News? Don't Blame Americans," *Detroit Free Press*, May 4, 2005.

[28] Local news, Michigan Radio, May 3, 2005.

[29] "Free Press Editorial Board interview with Jennifer Granholm," *Detroit Free Press*, February 10, 2005.

[30] Ibid.

[31] Dawson Bell, "The First First Gentleman," *Detroit Free Press*, March 6, 2005.

CHAPTER 7

[1] John McCain with Mark Salter, *Why Courage Matters: The Way a Braver Life*. New York: Random House, 2004, p. 198.

[2] "Paul Klebnikov" (obituary), *The Economist*, July 17, 2004

[3] Ibid.

[4] Steve Forbes, "Paul Klebnikov, 1963–2004," *Forbes*, August 16, 2004.

[5] "Paul Klebnikov" (obituary), *The Economist*, July 17, 2004; "Chechen 'Ordered Forbes [Reporter] Killing,'" CNN.com, June 16, 2005.

[6] "Paul Klebnikov" (obituary), *The Economist*, July 17, 2004.

[7] Steve Forbes, "Paul Klebnikov, 1963–2004," *Forbes*, August 16, 2004.

[8] Robert F. Worth, "An American Aid Worker Is Killed in Her Line of Duty," *New York Times*, April 18, 2005; *NewsHour with Jim Lehrer*, PBS, April 18, 2005.

[9] Peter Bergen, "World Knew Her Simply as Marla," CNN Online, April 19, 2005; Simon Robinson, "Appreciation: Marla Ruzicka, 1977–2005," *Time Online*, April 18, 2005.

[10] Peter Bergen, "World Knew Her Simply as Marla," CNN Online, April 19, 2005; Robert F. Worth, "An American Aid Worker Is Killed in Her Line of Duty," *New York Times*, April 18, 2005.

[11] Robert Coram, *Boyd: The Fighter Pilot Who Changed the Art of War*. Boston: Little, Brown, 2002.

[12] Scott Krisner, "One Tough Assignment," *Fast Company*, September 2004; 2004 Annual Report for Tyco.

[13] Cheryl Dahle, "On Thin Ice," *Fast Company*, September 2004.

[14] John McCain with Mark Salter, "In Search of Courage," *Fast Company*, September 2004 (adapted from *Why Courage Matters*, by John McCain with Mark Salter. New York: Random House, 2004).

[15] Chris Matthews interview with John McCain, *Hardball*, MSNBC, April 14, 2005; Chris Matthews interview with Jane Fonda, *Hardball*, MSNBC, April 15, 2005.

John McCain with Mark Salter, *Faith of My Fathers*. New York: Random House, 1999 (2000 paperback edition), pp. 188–212, 311.

pp. 232–238, 337–349.

[18] John McCain with Mark Salter, *Worth Fighting For*. New York: Random House, 2002 (2003 paperback edition), pp. 7, 32–33, 49–63.

[19] Ibid., pp. 54–56.

[20] Ibid., pp. 85–99.

[21] Ibid., pp. 59–61, 160–205.

[22] John McCain with Mark Salter, "In Search of Courage," *Fast Company*, September 2004.

[23] Larry King interview with John McCain, *Larry King Live*, CNN, May 21, 2004.

[24] Chris Matthews interview with John McCain, *Hardball*, MSNBC, April 14, 2005.

[25] Larry King interview with John McCain, *Larry King Live*, CNN, May 21, 2004.

[26] Charles Gibson interview with John McCain, *Good Morning America*, ABC, March 10, 2004.

[27] Associated Press, citing comments made by John McCain on ABC's *This Week*, March 20, 2005.

[28] Russell Baker, "Review of *Worth Fighting For*," *New York Review of Books*; cited on book jacket.

[29] John McCain with Mark Salter, *Worth Fighting For*. New York: Random House, 2002 (2003 paperback edition), pp. 62–63, 113–115.

CHAPTER 8

[1] Charlie Rose, "Q&A with Meg Whitman," E-commerce, www.business.cisco.com.

[2] Steve Weiberg, "De La Salle Team Keeps Win Streak in Check," *USA Today*, August 30, 2004.

[3] Don Wallace, "The Soul of a Sports Machine," *Fast Company*, October 2003.

[4] Ibid.

[5] Ibid.

[6] Ibid.

[7] Steve Weiberg, "De La Salle Team Keeps Win Streak in Check," *USA Today*, August 30, 2004.

[8] Ibid.

[9] Mitch Stephens, "De La Salle Beaten at Its Own Game," *San Francisco Chronicle*, September 6, 2004.

[10] Jim Goodnight, "The Experts Guide to Success in 2003," *Business 2.0*, December 2002.

[11] This profile, except where noted, is based on materials found in the *60 Minutes* profile that aired April 20, 2003 (rebroadcast of October 2002 presentation), as well as SAS's corporate Web site, www.sas.com.

[12] I would like to thank Gene Schutt for his development of this model. Quotes are excerpted from an interview with the author on March 16, 2005.

[13] Keith McNaughton, "Red, White & Bold," *Newsweek*, April 25, 2005.

[14] The change model formula is attributed to David Gleicher and cited in Richard Beckhard and Reuben T. Harris, *Organizational Transitions*. Reading, MA: AddisonWesley, 1987.

[15] David H. Freedman, *Corps Business: The Management Principles of the U.S. Marines*. New York: Harper Business, 2000, pp. 109–114.

[16] Rosabeth Moss Kanter, *Confidence*. New York: CrownBusiness, 2004, p. 3.

[17] This section on confidence first appeared in an article I wrote. John Baldoni "A Matter of Confidence," *CIO.com*, April 11, 2005; used with permission.

[18] Rosabeth Moss Kanter, *Confidence*. New York: CrownBusiness, 2004, pp. 291–321.

[19] Bevin Alexander, *How Wars Are Won*. New York: Crown, 2002, pp. 302–306.

[20] Victor Davis Hanson, *Carnage and Culture: Landmark Battles in the Rise of Western Power*. New York: Anchor Books, 2001 (2002 paperback edition), pp. 79–90.

[21] Quotes and facts related to the technology meltdown come from Patrick Dillon, "Peerless Leader; Perceptive, Adaptable, and Remarkably Low-Key, eBay Chief Executive Meg Whitman Rides e-Tail's Hottest Segment—The Global Garage Sale Called Peer-to-Peer," *Christian Science Monitor*, March 10, 2004.

[22] Ibid.

[23] Ibid.

[24] Charlie Rose, "Q&A with eBay's Meg Whitman," *iQ Magazine*, July-August 2001.

[25] Ibid.

[26] Nick Wingfield, "Auctioneer to the World," *Wall Street Journal*, August 5, 2004.

[27] Charlie Rose, "Q&A with eBay's Meg Whitman," *iQ Magazine*, July-August 2001.

[28] Quote attributed to *Forbes* magazine, cited in Patrick Dillon, "Peerless Leader; Perceptive, Adaptable, and Remarkably Low-Key, eBay Chief Executive Meg Whitman Rides e-Tail's Hottest Segment—The Global Garage Sale Called Peer-to-Peer," *Christian Science Monitor*, March 10, 2004.

[29] Ibid.

[30] Meg Whitman, "Best Advice I Ever Got," *Fortune*, March 21, 2005.

[31] Nick Wingfield, "Auctioneer to the World," *Wall Street Journal*, August 5, 2004.

[32] Laura Sydell, Profile: Internet Company eBay Not Growing as Quickly as It Used To, *Morning Edition*, NPR, June 14, 2005; "Meg and the Power of Many—eBay," *The Economist*, June 11, 2005.

[33] Nick Wingfield, "Auctioneer to the World," *Wall Street Journal*, August 5, 2004.

[34] Meg Whitman, "Best Advice I Ever Got," *Fortune*, March 21, 2005.

[35] Patrick Dillon, "Peerless Leader; Perceptive, Adaptable, and Remarkably Low-Key, eBay Chief Executive Meg Whitman Rides e-Tail's Hottest Segment—The Global Garage Sale Called Peer-to-Peer," *Christian Science Monitor*, March 10, 2004.

[36] Charlie Rose, "Q&A with eBay's Meg Whitman," *iQ Magazine*, July-August 2001.

CHAPTER 9

[1] Kenneth Turan, "Crossroads: Steve Spielberg," *Los Angeles Times*, December 28, 1998; Lester D. Friedman and Brent Notbohm (eds.), *Steven Spielberg Interviews*. Jackson, MS: University of Mississippi Press, 2000, p. 222.

[2] George P. Laszlo, "Southwest Comes First by Putting Customers Second," *Human Resource Management International Digest*, July–August 1999.

[3] Steven Oberbeck, "Southwest Airlines CEO Herb Kelleher, a Known Practical Joker, Once Arm-Wrestled Another CEO to Settle a Dispute," *Salt Lake City Tribune*, December 19, 1993.

[4] George P. Laszlo, "Southwest Comes First by Putting Customers Second," *Human Resource Management International Digest*, July–August 1999.

[5] Greg Jaffe, "Trail by Fire: On Ground in Iraq, Capt. Ayers Writes His Own Playbook," *Wall Street Journal*, September 22, 2004.

[6] Noel Tichy and Eli Cohen, *The Leadership Engine*. New York: HarperCollins, 1997, pp. 53–56.

[7] Ibid., pp. 50–53.

[8] Robert A. Caro, *Master of the Senate: The Years of Lyndon Johnson*, Vol. 3. New York: Random House, 2002, pp. 401–403.

[9] David Helpern, "At Sea with Steven Spielberg," *Take One*, March-April 1974; Lester D. Friedman and Brent Notbohm (eds.), *Steven Spielberg Interviews*. Jackson, MS: University of Mississippi Press, 2000, p. 4.

[10] Stephen J. Dubner, "Steven the Good," *New York Times*, February 14, 1999; Lester D. Friedman and Brent Notbohm (eds.), *Steven Spielberg Interviews*. Jackson, MS: University of Mississippi Press, 2000, pp. 223–224.

[11] Ibid., pp. 122–124, 223; Glenn Collins, "Spielberg Films *The Color Purple*," *New York Times*, December 15, 1985.

[12] Anthony Breznican, "Spielberg's Family Values," *USA Today*, June 24, 2005.

[13] Stephen J. Dubner, "Steven the Good," *New York Times*, February 14, 1999; Lester D. Friedman and Brent Notbohm (eds.), *Steven Spielberg Interviews*. Jackson, MS: University of Mississippi Press, 2000, p. 224.

[14] Joseph McBride, *Steven Spielberg*. New York: Simon & Schuster, 1997, pp. 422–441.

[15] David M. Halbfinger, "Next: Spielberg's Biggest Gamble," *New York Times*, July 1, 2005.

[16] "How Well Mr. Spielberg Wears a Suit," *The Economist*, July 30, 1998.

[17] Ibid.; Anthony Breznican, "Spielberg's Family Values," *USA Today*, June 24, 2005.

[18] Kate Kelley and Merissa Marr, "DreamWorks SKG May Go to Universal," *Wall Street Journal,* July 28, 2005 [sale of DW-SKG].

[19] Stephen J. Dubner, "Steven the Good," *New York Times*, February 14, 1999; Lester D. Friedman and Brent Notbohm (eds.), *Steven Spielberg Interviews*. Jackson, MS: University of Mississippi Press, 2000, p. 237.

[20] Michael Sragow, "A Conversation with Steven Spielberg," *Rolling Stone*, July 22, 1982; Lester D. Friedman and Brent Notbohm (eds.), *Steven Spielberg Interviews*. Jackson, MS: University of Mississippi Press, 2000, p. 108.

[21] Ibid., p. 228.

[22] Ibid., pp. 230, 234.

[23] Ibid., p. 223.

Index

About the Author

John Baldoni combines an extensive background in business communications with training and management development to help corporate clients develop their communications, learning, and leadership skills. His clientele includes leading global companies such as Ford, Kellogg's, and Pfizer. Baldoni, a popular author and keynote speaker on leadership, has been featured or quoted in many publications, including the *New York Times*, *USA Today*, the *Chicago Tribune*, *Investor's Business Daily*, and *Selling Power*. Readers are welcome to visit his leadership resource Web site www.johnbaldoni.com.